Does God Want Us to Be Happy?

Does *The Case for Biblical Happiness*

God Want

Us to Be

Happy?

RANDY ALCORN

TYNDALE
MOMENTUM®

The nonfiction imprint of
Tyndale House Publishers, Inc.

Visit Tyndale online at www.tyndale.com.

Visit Tyndale Momentum online at www.tyndalemomentum.com.

TYNDALE, *Tyndale Momentum*, and Tyndale's quill logo are registered trademarks of Tyndale House Publishers, Inc. The Tyndale Momentum logo is a trademark of Tyndale House Publishers, Inc. Tyndale Momentum is the nonfiction imprint of Tyndale House Publishers, Inc., Carol Stream, Illinois.

Does God Want Us to Be Happy?: The Case for Biblical Happiness

Designed by Eva M. Winters

The author is grateful for the helpful counsel of the literary agency, WTA Services LLC, Franklin, TN.

For information about special discounts for bulk purchases, please contact Tyndale House Publishers at csresponse@tyndale.com, or call 1-800-323-9400.

ISBN 978-1-4964-3257-5 (hc)

Printed in China

25	24	23	22	21	20	19
7	6	5	4	3	2	1

Contents

CHAPTER 1

DOES GOD CARE ABOUT OUR HAPPINESS?

IF YOU WERE TO ASK a roomful of people what God wants us to do, you'd likely get a wide range of answers.

Some people would say he wants us to obey him or to be holy. Others might claim he wants us to love people and stand up for peace and justice. But chances are, you wouldn't hear anyone say, "God wants us to be happy."

Most of us have a complicated relationship with happiness. We all want to be happy, but we may feel guilty about this longing. Isn't it selfish to pursue happiness? Isn't it more spiritual to frown than to smile?

In a world full of brokenness, we may wonder if happiness is a worthy pursuit. If we are seeking to follow Jesus, should this quest be written off as superficial and unspiritual?

Maybe you've been taught over the years that God cares about your holiness, not your happiness. This implies we have to choose between the two.

We've also heard that God calls us to joy, not happiness. According to innumerable sermons and books and blog posts, there's a big difference between joy, which is spiritual, and happiness, which is unspiritual. But does the Bible actually say this? Does God care about our happiness?

The answer might surprise you. Yes, God *does* care about our happiness. And he has gone to great lengths to prove it.

We Are Wired for Happiness

If you asked any group of people what they want out of life, chances are that most, if not all, would give some form of the same answer: "To be happy."

This inborn longing for happiness has been observed for thousands of years by theologians, philosophers, atheists, and agnostics.

Augustine (354–430), perhaps the most influential theologian in church history, wrote 1,600 years ago, "Every man, whatsoever his condition, desires to be happy."[1]

Nearly 1,300 years after Augustine, the French philosopher and mathematician Blaise Pascal (1623–1662) wrote, "All men seek happiness. This is without exception."[2]

Since then, countless others have observed the same.

Happiness Is Not Just a Secular Longing

Among Christ-followers, *happiness* was once a positive, desirable word.

Scottish churchman Thomas Boston (1676–1732) said, "Consider what man is. He is a creature that desires happiness, and cannot but desire it. The desire of happiness is woven into his nature, and cannot be eradicated. It is as natural for him to desire it as it is to breathe."[3]

Evangelist George Whitefield (1714–1770) said, "Is it the end of religion to make men happy, and is it not every one's privilege to be as happy as he can?"[4]

Whitefield once asked an audience, "Does [Jesus] want your heart only for the same end as the devil does, to make you miserable? No, he only wants you to believe on him, that you might be saved. This, this, is all the dear Savior desires, to make you happy, that you may leave your sins, to sit down eternally with him."[5]

Pastor Charles Spurgeon (1834–1892) said to his London congregation almost 150 years ago, "My dear Brothers and Sisters, if anybody in the world ought to be happy, we are the people. . . . How boundless our privileges! How brilliant our hopes!"[6]

Boston, Whitefield, and Spurgeon are just three Christian leaders among many throughout church history who knew that happiness is one of God's greatest gifts.

Let's be clear: we all know that happiness at the expense of others is wrong.

Is there selfish and superficial happiness? Sure. There's also selfish and superficial love, peace, loyalty, and trust. But we don't villainize these virtues just because they are sometimes misguided. Likewise, we shouldn't throw out Christ-centered and God-honoring happiness with the bathwater of self-centered happiness.

There's Good News about Happiness

If we want to be happy but God *doesn't* want us to be happy, wouldn't that be bad news?

The gospel is called the "good news of happiness" (Isaiah 52:7, ESV, NASB). Then why do Christians today often say things like "God wants you blessed, not happy"[7] and "God doesn't want you to be happy. God wants you to be holy"?[8]

Any message that God doesn't want us to be happy undermines the "good news of happiness" Jesus came to bring us. Compelling biblical evidence and a long history of Christ-followers have affirmed that our God is pro-happiness.

What if a happy God made us for happiness, and therefore our desire to be happy is inseparable from our longing for God?

What if God wired his image bearers for happiness before sin entered the world?

What if wanting happiness isn't the problem, but looking for happiness in sin is?

What if our desire to be happy can be properly redirected to God and all that he wants for us?

How might this perspective on happiness change our approach to life, parenting, church, ministry, business, sports, entertainment, and everything else?

Since unhappy Christians make the gospel unattractive, wouldn't the gospel become contagiously appealing if Christians embraced happiness in Jesus?

A Good Father Delights in His Children's Happiness

How many of us have ever heard a sermon, read a book, had a discussion about, or meditated on God's happiness? In fact, we're often taught to do exactly the opposite—to squelch our longing for happiness (which will never work).

The resulting silence about or contradiction of biblical revelation about one of God's great attributes is an immense loss to individuals and families, as well as to the church as a whole.

The title of this book is ironic. If we were thinking correctly, we would naturally wonder, *Why would anyone even ask whether God wants his people to be happy?*

Some unbelievers might be perplexed by the question "Does God want us to be happy?" If they *did* believe in a good God, surely they'd suppose he would value his children's happiness. *What good father wouldn't?*

Have you ever met a loving, devoted human father who doesn't want his children to be happy? Sure, he wouldn't want them to sacrifice personal integrity or virtue. But he knows that not having those things will never make them happy anyway! He wants them to make good and right choices that result in their long-term happiness.

The question "Does God want us to be happy?" makes sense to many of us only because we have been indoctrinated to believe he doesn't. That's what I was taught after becoming a Christian as a teenager. Millions of others have been taught the same.

I'm delighted to say that the Bible itself, along with the beliefs of people throughout church history, have liberated me from this misconception.

There's a Right Kind of Happiness

Many Christians live in daily sadness, anger, anxiety, or loneliness, thinking these feelings are inevitable, given their circumstances. Maybe you're one of them. We can lose joy over traffic jams, a stolen credit card, or increased gas prices. We can read Scripture with blinders on, missing the reasons for happiness expressed on nearly every page. But it doesn't have to be that way!

So let's explore this Christ-centered happiness further and see what God's Word and his people have to say about it.

My hope is that this book will open your eyes to the fact that the answer to "Does God want us to be happy?" is a resounding "Yes!" And my prayer is that you would thrive in this knowledge and unapologetically seek happiness in Jesus and in the wonders of his grace and his gifts.

CHAPTER 2

IS GOD HAPPY?

ANGLICAN BISHOP J. C. RYLE (1816–1900) wrote, "Happiness is what all mankind want to obtain—the desire for it is deeply planted in the human heart."[1]

If this desire is "deeply planted" in our hearts, then who planted it? Fallen people? The devil? Or, as J. C. Ryle believed, our Creator?

Our answer to that question will dramatically affect the way we see the world. If we believe God is happy, then doesn't it stand to reason that he would create us with the desire and capacity to be happy?

As we've seen, the gospel of salvation in the Messiah is prophesied as the "good news of happiness" (Isaiah 52:7). The angels proclaimed to the shepherds "good news of great joy" (Luke 2:10). The degree of happiness in the good news is dependent on the degree of happiness possessed by the originator and sender of that good news—God himself.

To be godly is to resemble God. If God were unhappy, we'd need to pursue unhappiness, which sounds as fun as cultivating an appetite for gravel.

Fortunately, however, God doesn't condemn or merely tolerate our desire to be happy; he *gave* us that longing. Through the Cross, he granted us the grounds and capacity to be happy forever. He encourages us here and now to find happiness in the very place it comes from—him.

Happiness Began with the Triune God

In one sense, the idea that happiness began with God isn't exactly right. Because if happiness is part of who God is, then happiness didn't "begin" at all—it has always been, since God has always been.

In his book *Delighting in the Trinity*, Michael Reeves writes, "The Trinity is the governing center of all Christian belief, the truth that shapes and beautifies all others. The Trinity is the cockpit of all Christian thinking."[2] Yet strangely, the Trinity is rarely discussed in most Christian books on joy or happiness.

Twice in Matthew's Gospel—at Jesus' baptism and at the Transfiguration—we see extraordinary exhibitions of the triune God's happiness:

When Jesus was baptized . . . behold, the heavens
were opened to him, and he saw the Spirit of
God descending like a dove and coming to rest
on him; and behold, a voice from heaven said,
"This is my beloved Son, with whom I am well
pleased."

MATTHEW 3:16-17

The Father's and the Holy Spirit's participation in this
event demonstrates their approval of Jesus and their happiness in him.

At the Transfiguration, the Father's statement is
repeated: "This is my beloved Son, with whom I am well
pleased; listen to him" (Matthew 17:5).

In Isaiah's prophecy about the coming of Jesus, the
Father says, "Behold my servant, whom I uphold, my
chosen, in whom my soul delights" (Isaiah 42:1). For
the Father to be well pleased and delighted with his Son
means he finds great happiness in him.

Likewise, the Son and the Holy Spirit had every reason
for total delight in each other and with the Father from
before the dawn of time (see John 17:24 and 1 Peter 1:20).

Steve DeWitt writes, "Before you ever had a happy
moment, or your great-grandparents had a happy
moment, or Adam and Eve had a happy moment—before
the universe was even created—God the Father and God

the Son and God the Spirit were enjoying a perfect and robust relational delight in one another."[3]

God's communal happiness within himself has significant implications for our own happiness. It means happiness began long before the first human experienced it. It also explains how God could be displeased with his creatures and their sin without disrupting his innate happiness.

Does the Bible Really Say God Is Happy?

Yes, it certainly does! Many times Scripture states that God experiences delight and pleasure. But sadly, in some cases when it affirms God's happiness, readers of English Bibles don't understand what the original language was communicating.

The apostle Paul wrote of "the gospel of the glory of the blessed [*makarios*] God with which I have been entrusted" (1 Timothy 1:11). Later in the same book, God is referred to as "he who is the blessed [*makarios*] and only Sovereign, the King of kings and Lord of lords" (6:15).

In 1611, when the King James Version translators chose the word *blessed* in verses like these, it meant "happy"! Even two centuries after the KJV was translated, people still understood *blessed* to mean "happy."

For example, Charles Spurgeon, a renowned nineteenth-century preacher, commented about this connection between *blessed* and *happy*. He said of 1 Timothy 1:11, "The Gospel . . . is the Gospel of happiness. It is called, 'the glorious Gospel of the blessed God.' A more correct translation would be, 'the happy God.' Well, then, adorn the Gospel by being happy!"[4]

While "blessed" was once a good translation, today it fails to convey the connotation of happiness that the original word held for Paul's readers.

What's the Source of Happiness?

Paul didn't simply talk about the gospel; he talked about its source: "the happy God." This good news comes from not just any god but the one true *happy* God.

Occam's razor is the philosophical rule that the simplest explanation is most likely true. In 1 Timothy 1:11, the simplest explanation is that, writing under the inspiration of God's Spirit, *Paul called God happy precisely because God is happy!*

Once you realize God's happiness, you see it everywhere in Scripture. For instance, in Christ's story of the Prodigal Son, the elder brother resents his father for happily celebrating his brother's repentance. The father explains, "But we had to celebrate and be happy, because your brother was dead, but now he is alive; he was lost, but now he has been found" (Luke 15:32, GNT).

Why did the father say he *had* to celebrate and be happy?

God only has to do what's true to his nature—his happiness compels celebration. He grieves over sin—even to the point of dying on a cross to restore his relationship with his children. When they repent, he throws a party and all Heaven rejoices (see Luke 15:7; 22-24). *This all transpires because God is happy!* When I've shared from Scripture the truth of God's happiness, people who have long been Christians are often initially skeptical, assuming this is a modern attempt to twist the Bible's meaning. But once they see this ancient, biblically solid truth, they're both surprised and delighted.

Many Scriptures Assume God's Happiness

We are told, "Delight yourself in the LORD" (Psalm 37:4). Do you take delight in people who are not delightful?

"May all those who seek you be happy and rejoice in you!" (Psalm 40:16, NET). Could we be happy in God if God were not happy? Could we rejoice in him if he were not joyful?

Psalm 2:12 offers a clear picture of the happiness of those who trust God:

- Happy are all who go to him for protection. (GNT)
- All those who take refuge in Him are happy. (HCSB)

The oldest and most literal English translations render the verse this way:

- Happy be all they, who trust in him. (WYC)
- O the happiness of all trusting in Him! (YLT)

How could we become happy by taking refuge in a God who is not happy?

Other verses describe the happiness offered God's people:

- Happy is the person whom the LORD does not consider guilty. (Psalm 32:2, NCV)
- Happy is the nation whose God is Yahweh. (Psalm 33:12, HCSB)
- Happy are those whom you choose. (Psalm 65:4, NRSV, GNT)

These passages don't directly state, "God is happy." But they make sense only if he is. When was the last time you were made happy by an unhappy person?

We are to be holy because God is (see 1 Peter 1:16). We should be happy for the same reason—because God is.

How Can God Be Happy When There's So Much Sin?

We know that God is unhappy with sin, and there's so much sin in the world. So isn't he unhappy all the time?

God's unhappiness is specifically directed at sin.

Therefore, it is temporary, because sin itself is a temporary aberration, decisively and eternally dealt with by Christ.

Happiness, in contrast, is the underlying nature of the timeless God. His happiness is eternal and constant. It preceded sin's birth and will forever continue after sin's death. He who was happy before the world began will be happy in the world to come, and he is happy now.

I'm convinced that in the new universe—called in Scripture the New Heaven and the New Earth—the attribute of God's happiness will overflow everywhere we look. The God who delights to make us happy tells us, "My people will be happy forever because of the things I will make" (Isaiah 65:18, NCV).

Upon their deaths, Christ-followers won't hear, "Go and submit to your master's harshness" but "Come and join in your master's happiness!" (Matthew 25:21, CJB).

The literal translation is, "Enter into your master's happiness." We can only enter into what already exists. To enter into our master's happiness means we don't have to muster up our own happiness. Rather, God invites us to participate in his own infinite happiness, which has unlimited room for the happiness of his creatures.

Once we comprehend the enormity of God's happiness, anticipating those amazing words "Enter into my happiness" can sustain us through every heartbreak and challenge in our present lives.

No wonder the devil doesn't want us to believe in God's happiness! He knows how completely it would thwart his attempts to make us view life with a dismal and downtrodden perspective.

God's Happiness Is Attractive

When we recognize that God is happy, we see how his happiness overflows in all he does.

If your grumpy neighbor asks, "What are you up to?" you'll see the question as suspicious and condemning. But if your cheerful neighbor asks the same thing, you'll smile and talk about your plans. We interpret people's words according to how we perceive their character and outlook. So it is with our view of God.

If we think of God as unhappy—and many sincere Christians do—we will interpret his words in Scripture accordingly. When he tells us not to do certain things, we'll think he's trying to keep us from happiness. But if we know God to be happy, we will understand that he tells us to avoid things because, like a loving parent who warns a child to stay away from the highway, he wants us to be wise and happy.

Christians are often told to spend time with God in the Bible and through prayer and in church. This is good counsel, but the unspoken question sometimes is, "Why would I want to spend time with an unhappy God who cares about my obedience but not my happiness?"

As the only infinite being in the universe, God has within himself not only unlimited holiness, love, and goodness, but also unlimited joy, gladness, and delight.

Happiness is attractive and contagious. Infinite happiness is infinitely attractive. Those who believe God is happy will *want* to know him better.

To think of God as not only good but good natured is paradigm shifting. Being drawn to his quality of happiness, like any who fall in love, we will be eager to spend time with him and learn more about his other attributes.

Isn't it time we not only acknowledge but enthusiastically celebrate what the Bible has said all along about the "good news of happiness" (Isaiah 52:7), and the glorious gospel of the happy God (see 1 Timothy 1:11)?

CHAPTER 3

WHO WAS THE HAPPIEST PERSON IN HUMAN HISTORY?

SEVERAL YEARS AGO my wife led a women's Bible study discussion on a lesson she'd written about the happiness of Jesus. One woman who'd grown up in church was startled. She shared how horrified she'd once been to see a picture of Jesus smiling. Why? Because she believed it was blasphemous to portray Jesus as happy!

This woman is not alone. Ask a random group of believers and unbelievers, "Who is the happiest human being who ever lived?" and very few, if any, would give the correct answer: Jesus.

You might be surprised by the claim that the life of Jesus was marked by happiness, but I believe this can be clearly proven from Scripture.

Scripture Affirms Christ's Happiness

Christ is called "the wisdom of God" (1 Corinthians 1:24). Jesus referred to himself as "wisdom" when he said, "The Son of Man came eating and drinking, and they say, 'Look at him! A glutton and a drunkard, a friend of tax collectors and sinners!' Yet wisdom is justified by her deeds" (Matthew 11:19).

It's significant that Jesus calls wisdom "her," not him. This immediately resonated with his scripturally literate audience, making them think of "Lady Wisdom," depicted in Proverbs 8 as full of happiness and delight in God the Father.

Puritan theologian John Gill (1697–1771) said Proverbs 8 is about "Christ, under the name of Wisdom."[1] English preacher Charles Bridges (1794–1869) claimed that the wisdom referred to in Proverbs 8 is "the voice of the Son of God."[2] Modern Anglican scholar Derek Kidner (1913–2008) took this position,[3] as does Old Testament professor Tremper Longman III: "Jesus claims [in Matthew 11:19] that his behavior represents the behavior of Woman Wisdom herself."[4]

Why does all of this matter? Because Proverbs 8 is a stunning statement of the eternal happiness of God's Son.

Speaking of the Father, this ancient and eternal Wisdom says, "When he established the heavens, I was there. . . . When he marked out the foundations of the earth, then I was beside him, like a master workman" (verses 27, 29-30).

Wisdom—clearly not just an attribute, but a being—says, "I was constantly at his side. I was filled with delight day after day, rejoicing always in his presence, rejoicing in his whole world and delighting in mankind" (verses 30-31, NIV). The Hebrew word translated "rejoicing" here could be accurately rendered "laughing" or "playing."[5]

The Common English Bible captures these words of God's all-wise Son: "I was *having fun, smiling* before him all the time, *frolicking* with his inhabited earth and *delighting* in the human race" (Proverbs 8:30-31, emphasis added). The Good News Translation says, "I was his daily source of joy, always happy in his presence—happy with the world and pleased with the human race."

Creation is attributed to Christ (see John 1:1-3 and Colossians 1:16). But here he's seen as playfully interacting with his Father and his creation. What an amazing portrayal of the pre-incarnate happiness of Jesus!

Jesus Was a Man of Sorrows *and* a Man of Happiness

People often reject the idea of Jesus being happy by quoting from Isaiah 53:3: "He was despised and rejected by men, a man of sorrows and acquainted with grief."

In order to understand this verse, we need to grasp

the sense in which Jesus was a man of sorrows. When Jesus, the eternally happy one, came to Earth, he entered a world under the Curse, plagued by sin. He saw and knew suffering and distress, to the point that in Gethsemane his agony was so intense his capillaries burst (see Luke 22:44).

But the context of Isaiah 53 shows that the Messiah is called "a man of sorrows" not generally, but specifically in relationship to his suffering and sacrificial work. Going to the cross, Jesus said, "My soul is deeply grieved to the point of death" (Mark 14:34, NASB).

But Jesus lived more than twelve thousand days, and all this intense sorrow happened in by far the worst twenty-four hours of his life.

Given the price Jesus paid for our sins, does being "a man of sorrows" in his atoning work contradict the notion that Jesus, overall, was happy?

Absolutely not! Sorrow and happiness can and do coexist within the same person. A person may be predominantly sad and occasionally happy, or predominantly happy and occasionally sad.

Here's how Scripture describes Jesus during the darkest day of his life: "For the *joy* that was set before him [he] endured the cross, despising the shame, and is seated at the right hand of the throne of God" (Hebrews 12:2, emphasis added).

This means Jesus was conscious of and clinging to this joy that was ahead of him. What did that joy entail?

- the joy of pleasing the Father and the Holy Spirit
- the joy of redeeming his beloved people
- the joy of working together with the Spirit to sanctify his people
- the joy of granting his people entrance to Heaven
- the joy of saying to his people, "Well done" and "Come and share your master's happiness" (Matthew 25:23, NIV)
- the joy of granting his people positions of service in his Kingdom
- the joy of eternally reigning as the "last Adam" over the New Earth (1 Corinthians 15:45)
- the joy of seeing his people raised from the dead and watching them celebrate and laugh, never to weep again

Jesus understood that the basis for his sorrow was temporary, while the basis for his gladness is permanent.

Jesus knew unbounded happiness before the dawn of time, and he knew it awaited him again in even greater measure!

The Early Church Knew Jesus Was Happy

The happiness of Jesus was a central preaching point in the early church. In the first-ever gospel message of the newborn church, the apostle Peter preached that Psalm 16 is about Christ: "David says concerning him, 'I saw the Lord always before me, for he is at my right hand that I may not be shaken; therefore my heart was *glad*, and my tongue *rejoiced*. . . . For you will not abandon my soul to Hades, or let your Holy One see corruption. . . . You will make me *full of gladness* with your presence'" (Acts 2:25-28, emphasis added). This effusive statement, attributed to the Messiah, affirms his happiness three times!

The passage Peter ascribed to Jesus includes Psalm 16:11: "In your presence there is fullness of joy; at your right hand are pleasures forevermore." The New Life Version says, "Being with You is to be full of joy. In Your right hand there is happiness forever."

Psalm 45:6-7 is quoted in direct reference to the Messiah in Hebrews 1:8-9, where the Father says of his Son, "You have loved righteousness and hated wickedness; therefore God, your God, has anointed you with the oil of gladness beyond your companions."

Who are Jesus' companions in this passage? Given the context of Hebrews 1, where Jesus is portrayed as God incarnate, "companions" probably refers to all his fellow humans. This appears to be a direct affirmation that the gladness of Jesus exceeds that of all humans who have ever lived.

This understanding fits perfectly with the following verse (verse 10), which declares that Jesus is the creator. Hence, his image bearers—who have minds and creativity like his, only on an infinitely smaller scale—are also capable of finite happiness derivative of his own unlimited happiness.

Reflecting on Psalm 45 and Hebrews 1, John Piper writes, "Jesus Christ is the happiest being in the universe. His gladness is greater than all the angelic gladness of heaven. He mirrors perfectly the infinite, holy, indomitable mirth of his Father."[6]

Scripture commands us to follow in Jesus' footsteps (see 1 Peter 2:21). When we become convinced that our Savior walked this Earth not only experiencing suffering and sorrow but also doing so with an ancient yet forever-young happiness in his heart, it will result in a paradigm shift for us. We will be inspired to love him more deeply and follow him more cheerfully, and in the process "make the teaching about God our Savior attractive" (Titus 2:10, NIV).

The Christian life can be characterized by happiness because Jesus, who is the source and center and sustaining power of our lives, overflows with happiness.

Did Jesus Laugh?

We can't have a correct view of Jesus unless we embrace his happiness, which always includes laughter and a good sense of humor.

An evangelical pamphlet says, "Jesus never laughed."[7] True, the Bible never directly states that Jesus laughed, but that doesn't prove anything. We're told that the vast majority of what Jesus said and did is not recorded in Scripture (see John 20:30; 21:25).

Arguing that Jesus didn't laugh because the Bible doesn't mention it is like saying Jesus didn't breathe, yawn, sneeze, or run. We can safely assume he did those things because Scripture tells us Jesus was fully human (see Hebrews 2:14-18).

Did Jesus joke with his friends? The better question is, *Why wouldn't he?* Jesus knew the truth of Solomon's words: there is "a time to weep, and a time to laugh; a time to mourn, and a time to dance" (Ecclesiastes 3:4). Surely we should believe, since Jesus was fully human, born into a culture alive with feasts and festivals, that he did all of these!

One of the psalms that Jesus would have meditated on from his childhood says, "When the LORD brought us back to Jerusalem, it was like a dream! How we laughed, how we sang for joy! . . . Indeed he did great things for us; how happy we were!" (Psalm 126:1-3, GNT).

Laughter is not only human, it's explicitly biblical and pleasing to God. It's therefore inconceivable that Jesus didn't laugh! Did humor come into the universe as the result of sin? No. Did Satan invent humor? Of course not. We have a sense of humor because, as his image bearers, we're similar to God, who enjoys laughter and who created our capacity to laugh and the wonderful feeling it gives us.

Did Jesus Have a Sense of Humor?

The humor of Jesus becomes obvious if we understand his culture and his engaging presence. What people found funny in that time and place was not stand-up comedy but hyperbole.

The *Dictionary of Biblical Imagery* says, "Jesus was a master of wordplay, irony and satire, often with an element of humor intermixed."[8] It adds, "The most characteristic form of Jesus' humor was the preposterous exaggeration."[9]

Such exaggeration isn't falsehood, of course. Someone might say, "I went to the store at four o'clock in the afternoon, and a million other people had the same idea." The speaker isn't lying; he's just being funny. Many of Jesus' statements are, by design, happily outrageous.

Jesus told of a wealthy man who hands over five talents to a servant (see Matthew 25). That amount was the equivalent of nearly a hundred years' wages.[10] That would be like saying, "So this businessman gave his employee five million dollars to invest . . ."

Jesus spoke of a king who loaned one of his servants ten thousand talents (see Matthew 18:23-35)—a ludicrous amount, since the average person earned just one talent every twenty years.[11] Jesus deliberately painted an absurd picture that says, "Our debt to God is infinite."

Consider when Jesus asked, "Why do you see the speck that is in your brother's eye, but do not notice the log that is in your own eye?" (Matthew 7:3). Theologian and chaplain Elton Trueblood (1900–1994) noticed Christ's humor for the first time when he was reading this passage aloud and his young son burst into laughter at the picture of a log in someone's eye.[12]

Jesus told a parable about the wise man who built his house on rock and the foolish man who built his house on sand (see Matthew 7:24-27). The moment they heard about the man building on sand, the audience would have cringed and laughed, knowing where the story was going!

When Jesus told the parable about sewing a piece of new cloth on an old garment (see Luke 5:36), every housewife would have smiled knowingly at that ill-advised plan.

When he said, "Neither is new wine put into old wineskins. If it is, the skins burst and the wine is spilled and the skins are destroyed" (Matthew 9:17), no doubt people in the crowd grinned and nodded, having learned that very thing the hard way. Fermentation expands wine, causing a sealed wineskin to explode.

Consider this example: "If the householder had known at what hour the thief was coming, he would have been awake and would not have left his house to be broken into" (Luke 12:39, RSVCE). Imagine a thief and a home-owner coordinating a robbery!

Jesus asked, "Is a lamp brought in to be put under a basket, or under a bed, and not on a stand?" (Mark 4:21). Lamps in Jesus' day had open flames, and a bed was a straw mattress. The imagery is absurd, and therefore hilarious.

Referring to the religious leaders, Jesus said, "They are blind guides. And if the blind lead the blind, both will fall into a pit" (Matthew 15:14). The irony of a self-declared guide who can't see certainly would have prompted laughter.

On another occasion Jesus said to the Pharisees, "You blind guides, straining out a gnat and swallowing a camel!" (Matthew 23:24). Straining out a gnat would be hard for anyone—but impossible for the blind. And what's more ridiculous than swallowing a camel? This exaggeration surely evoked laughter—especially because it involved a put-down of the arrogant Pharisees who delighted in denigrating the "little people."

Jesus referred to Herod as "that fox" (Luke 13:32). Since a fox is cunning, this may appear to be a compliment, but it wouldn't have been lost on the crowd that those pointy-eared varmints were nuisances, not terrors. Jesus was poking fun at an immoral, murderous tyrant by comparing him not to a lion or a bear but to a fox! Imagine people telling their friends, "You won't believe what Jesus called Herod!"

When reading "Do not . . . cast your pearls before swine" (Matthew 7:6, NKJV), a modern reader might wonder why Jesus would say something so outlandish. But Christ's tongue-in-cheek comment is a warning not to do the spiritual equivalent of such an utterly ridiculous thing.

"When you give to the needy," Jesus told people, "sound no trumpet before you, as the hypocrites do" (Matthew 6:2). Of course, no one would literally blow a trumpet as they gave; instead they would find subtle ways to make their philanthropy visible. But Jesus used the hyperbolic trumpet to poke fun at self-congratulatory actions. Can't you hear people laughing?

Jesus may also have laughed at his own human limitations. He didn't sin or make foolish decisions, but I suspect he sometimes tripped or spilled milk.

God's Son brought into the world not only the grace and truth of God but also his happiness, humor, and laughter. On the New Earth, as we play and feast, joke and tell stories together, always looking to our Redeemer, I truly believe that no smile will be bigger, no laugh louder, and no happiness more contagious than his.

CHAPTER 4

WHAT ARE SOME
CHRISTIAN MYTHS
ABOUT HAPPINESS?

IN 1629 EDWARD LEIGH (1602–1671) wrote, "The happiness of man consists in the enjoying of God. All other things are no . . . means of happiness or helps to it, then as we see and taste God in them."[1]

This wise Puritan was saying that the very things God has given us to make us happy succeed in doing so only when we first and foremost find our happiness in God.

Puritan preacher Thomas Brooks (1608–1680) said, "God is the author of all true happiness; he is the donor of all true happiness. . . . He that hath him for his God, for his portion, is the only happy man in the world."[2]

English evangelist John Wesley (1703–1791) said, "When we first know Christ . . . then it is that happiness begins; happiness real, solid, substantial."³ Wesley also said, "None but a Christian is happy; none but a real inward Christian."⁴

While happiness is what we all want and what believers throughout the centuries affirmed is a good desire when it's sought in Christ, countless modern Christians have been taught various myths about happiness. We must address those myths in order to answer the question "Does God want us to be happy?"

Is Happiness a Matter of Chance?

It's common to hear objections to the word *happy* based on its etymology, or history. The most frequent objection is articulated by one commentator: "Happy comes from the word 'hap,' meaning 'chance.' It is therefore incorrect to translate [the Greek word *makarios*] as 'happy.'"⁵

This argument may sound valid, but it's baseless. Our language is full of words long detached from their original meanings. *Enthusiasm* originally meant "in the gods," but if I say you're enthusiastic, I'm not suggesting that you are a polytheist. Likewise, our word *nice* comes from the Latin *nescius*, which means "ignorant." But we all know that's not what *nice* means today.

When people say they want to be happy, they are typically making no statement whatsoever about "chance." D. A. Carson argues in *Exegetical Fallacies*,

"The meaning of a word cannot be reliably determined by etymology."[6]

King James Version translators wouldn't have used *happy* and other forms of the root word *happiness* thirty-six times or translated *makarios* as some form of "happy" seventeen times if they thought its word history disqualified *happy* as a credible biblical word.

The fact is, the Puritans, Jonathan Edwards, John Wesley, Charles Spurgeon, and many others used the words *happy* and *happiness* frequently in biblical, theological, and Christ-centered contexts. When they called on believers to be happy, they weren't speaking of happenstance or chance, but of enduring delight and pleasure and good cheer in Jesus. They used *happy* and *happiness* because of their contemporary meaning: a glad and universally desired state of mind.

Does God Care Only about Our Holiness?

Some Christians see happiness as the virtual opposite of holiness. But Scripture says otherwise.

Consider Leviticus 9:24: "Fire came out from the presence of the LORD and consumed the burnt offering . . . on the altar. And when all the people saw it, they shouted for joy and fell facedown" (NIV).

The radically holy God sent down fire, and the people did *what*? They fell facedown . . . and "shouted for joy"!

This remarkable response flows from the utter holiness of submission combined with the utter happiness of praise.

To be holy is to see God as he is and to become like him, covered in Christ's righteousness. And since God's nature is to be happy (as we saw in chapter 2), the more like him we become in our sanctification, the happier we will be.

We see this link between happiness and holiness in many passages, including this one: "Let your priests be clothed with righteousness, and let your saints shout for joy" (Psalm 132:9).

Greek scholar J. B. Phillips (1906–1982) translated Revelation 20:6 this way: "Happy and holy is the one who shares in the first resurrection!" Similarly, the most literal English version, Young's Literal Translation, renders it "Happy and holy [is] he who is having part in the first rising again."

Most translations of this verse read "blessed and holy," with the result that modern readers (unaware that in old English *blessed* meant *happy*) understand the sentence as containing two adjectives of consecration. But when the Greek is rendered "happy and holy," readers can realize, *Wow, so those who know God are not only holy but also happy? Happiness is what I've been searching for! Maybe I should stop dividing my life into "church me," in which I try to be holy, and "world me," in which I seek to be happy.*

Any understanding of God is utterly false if it is incompatible with the lofty and infinitely holy view of God in Ezekiel 1:26-28 and Isaiah 6:1-4 and of Jesus in Revelation 1:9-18. God is decidedly and unapologetically anti-sin, but he is in no sense anti-happiness. Indeed, holiness is exactly what *secures* our happiness. Spurgeon said, "Holiness is the royal road to happiness. The death of sin is the life of joy."[7]

Holiness doesn't mean abstaining from pleasure; holiness means recognizing Jesus as the source of life's greatest pleasure.

Does Scripture Put Joy above Happiness?

Oswald Chambers (1874–1917), author of the excellent bestselling devotional *My Utmost for His Highest*, was one of the earliest Bible teachers to speak against happiness. He wrote, "Happiness is no standard for men and women because happiness depends on my being determinedly ignorant of God and His demands."[8]

After extensive research, I'm convinced that no biblical or historical basis whatsoever exists to define happiness as inherently sinful. Unfortunately, because Bible teachers such as Chambers saw people trying to find happiness in sin, they came to think that happiness isn't good and pursuing happiness is sinful.

Chambers said, "Joy is not happiness," and then

continued, "There is no mention in the Bible of happiness for a Christian, but there is plenty said about joy."[9]

That simply is not true. In the KJV, which Chambers used, Jesus tells his disciples, "If ye know these things, happy are ye if ye do them" (John 13:17). Speaking of faithful Christians, James said, "We count them happy which endure" (James 5:11). Peter said to fellow believers, "If ye suffer for righteousness' sake, happy are ye" and "If ye be reproached for the name of Christ, happy are ye" (1 Peter 3:14; 4:14).

Oswald Chambers also wrote, "Joy should not be confused with happiness. In fact, it is an insult to Jesus Christ to use the word happiness in connection with Him."[10]

I certainly respect Oswald Chambers, but statements like this are unfortunate and misleading. It's hard for me to conceive of a greater insult to Jesus than to effectively deny what Hebrews 1:9 reveals about his happy nature: "God, Your God, has anointed You with the oil of gladness above Your companions" (NASB).

It also seems insulting to say that the best Father in the universe doesn't want his children happy—especially when Father and Son and Spirit went to such great lengths to purchase our eternal happiness.

False claims that happiness is unbiblical are all too common: "Joy is in 155 verses in the KJV Bible, happiness isn't in the Bible."[11]

In reality, the Bible is a vast reservoir containing not dozens but hundreds of passages conveying happiness. In fact, I've looked at more than 2,700 Scripture passages where words such as *joy, happiness, gladness, merriment, pleasure, celebration, cheer, laughter, delight, jubilation, feasting, exultation,* and *celebration* are used. Throw in the words *blessed* and *blessing,* which often connote happiness (as we'll discuss in chapter 6), and the number increases.

The English Standard Version, which I often cite in this book, doesn't use the word *happy* nearly as often as many other translations, but it's still there:

- Happy are you, O Israel! Who is like you, a people saved by the LORD? (Deuteronomy 33:29)
- Judah and Israel were as many as the sand by the sea. They ate and drank and were happy. (1 Kings 4:20)
- How beautiful upon the mountains are the feet of him who brings good news, who publishes peace, who brings good news of happiness. (Isaiah 52:7)

Even without the word *happiness,* the concept is unmistakable in passages such as this one: "All the days of the afflicted are evil, but the cheerful of heart has a continual feast" (Proverbs 15:15).

Consider the Psalms, which reflect both great sorrow and great happiness:

- I will be happy and rejoice in you! I will sing praises to you, O sovereign One! (Psalm 9:2, NET)
- I will go to your altar, O God; you are the source of my happiness. I will play my harp and sing praise to you, O God, my God. (Psalm 43:4, GNT)
- Delight yourself in the LORD, and he will give you the desires of your heart. (Psalm 37:4)

What does "Delight yourself in the LORD" mean, if not "Be happy in God"? Scripture is clear that seeking happiness—or joy, gladness, delight, or pleasure—through sin is wrong and fruitless. But seeking happiness in him is good and right and God honoring.

This is a very small sampling of all that the Bible says about happiness.[12] But surely it's large enough to disprove the tragic misperception that God's Word doesn't talk about happiness.

CHAPTER 5

ARE JOY AND HAPPINESS AT ODDS WITH EACH OTHER?

WHILE RESEARCHING AND WRITING my book *Happiness*, I had dozens of nearly identical conversations.

Someone would ask, "What are you writing about?"

I'd respond, "Happiness."

Unbelievers were immediately interested. Believers typically gave me an odd look and responded warily, "Do you mean *joy*?"

A pastor friend wrote to tell me why it would be a big mistake to write a book about happiness. He told me what he'd been taught to think: "Happiness changes from moment to moment and is reflected by our moods and emotions. Joy is a spiritual peace and contentment that only comes from God. God's desire is not to make us happy in this life but to give us joy from our relationship with Christ."

Many people I've talked with believe that Scripture distinguishes between joy and happiness, and that the Bible depicts joy as godly and happiness as ungodly.

Is Happiness the Opposite of Joy?

A book on Christian ministry has a chapter called "Happiness vs. Joy." It says, "Joy and happiness are very different."[1]

In a chapter titled "Joy versus Happiness" another Christian author states, "Happiness is a feeling, while joy is a state of being."[2]

Another book claims, "Joy is distinctly a Christian word. . . . It is the reverse of happiness."[3]

In an article called "Jesus Doesn't Want You to Be Happy," the author states, "As you read through the gospels you'll see plenty of promises of joy, but none of happiness. And they are infinitely different things."[4]

Happiness is the *reverse* of joy? The two are *infinitely* different? The Bible makes no promise of happiness? Emphatic proclamations against happiness are so common among believers that many assume they must be true.

What is the scriptural, historical, or linguistic basis for making such statements? There simply is none! God makes no significant distinction between *joy* and *happiness*. They are synonyms!

Don't get me wrong. *Joy* is a great word, and I use it frequently. But there are other equally valid words with overlapping meanings, including *happiness*, *gladness*, *merriment*, *delight*, and *pleasure*. These are all part of what linguists call the same "semantic domain," or family of words. Depicting joy in contrast with happiness has obscured the true meaning of both words.

If you look in Hebrew and Greek lexicons at the many different words translated *joyful*, *glad*, *merry*, and *delighted*, you'll find that in nearly every case, these words are defined as "happy."

John Piper writes, "If you have nice little categories for 'joy is what Christians have' and 'happiness is what the world has,' you can scrap those when you go to the Bible, because the Bible is indiscriminate in its uses of the language of happiness and joy and contentment and satisfaction."[5]

Secular sources agree that happiness and joy are synonyms—much more alike than not. *Joy*, in Merriam-Webster's dictionary, is defined as "a feeling of great happiness" and "a source or cause of great happiness."[6] Every dictionary and thesaurus attests to the predominant overlap of meaning between happiness and joy.

Don't we instinctively know this? Think of our common expressions using the word *joy*:

- "He jumped for joy."
- "She's our pride and joy."
- "I wept for joy."

In each case, isn't joy obviously synonymous with happiness?

Joy Isn't Inherently Godly

Isaac Watts (1674–1748), who wrote "Joy to the World," also spoke of "carnal joys."[7]

Charles Spurgeon recognized the difference between false and true joy:

> Christ would not have us rejoice with the false
> joy of presumption, so He bares the sharp knife
> and cuts that joy away. Joy on a false basis would
> prevent us from having true joy.[8]

Someone can have Christ-centered happiness or Christ-denying happiness. The former will last forever; the latter has an exceedingly short shelf life.

Notice writer A. W. Tozer's (1897–1963) negative use of *joy* and positive use of *happiness* sixty years ago: "Human beings are busy trying to work up a joy of some sort. . . . They turn to television programs. But we still don't see the truly happy faces."[9] Tozer realized that artificial attempts at finding joy can't create the happiness that comes only from Christ.

There's a Biblical Link between Joy and Happiness

The following passages emphatically refute two common claims: (1) that the Bible doesn't mention or value or promise happiness and (2) that joy and happiness have contrasting meanings.

In fact, the Bible overflows with accounts of God's people being happy in him. Realize that these are not one-person paraphrases; rather, each of these translation teams consisted of Hebrew and Greek scholars who came to a consensus as to the best English renderings. (Emphasis has been added by the author.)

New International Version

- For the Jews it was a time of *happiness* and *joy*, gladness and honor. (Esther 8:16)
- May the righteous be glad and rejoice before God; may they be *happy* and *joyful*. (Psalm 68:3)
- This is what the LORD Almighty says: "The fasts . . . will become *joyful* and glad occasions and *happy* festivals for Judah." (Zechariah 8:19)

Holman Christian Standard Bible

- Don't you know that . . . the *joy* of the wicked has been brief and the *happiness* of the godless has lasted only a moment? (Job 20:4-5)
- *Happy* are the people who know the *joyful* shout; LORD, they walk in the light from your face. (Psalm 89:15)
- Then the young women will rejoice with dancing, while young and old men rejoice together. I will turn their mourning into *joy* . . . and bring *happiness* out of grief. (Jeremiah 31:13)

New Living Translation

- Give your father and mother *joy*! May she who gave you birth be *happy*. (Proverbs 23:25)
- Eat your food with *joy*, and drink your wine with a *happy* heart, for God approves of this! (Ecclesiastes 9:7)
- Be glad; rejoice forever in my creation! And look! I will create Jerusalem as a place of *happiness*. Her people will be a source of *joy*. (Isaiah 65:18)

God's Word

- You didn't serve the LORD your God with a *joyful* and *happy* heart when you had so much. (Deuteronomy 28:47)

- The people ransomed by the LORD . . . will come to Zion singing with *joy*. Everlasting *happiness* will be on their heads as a crown. They will be glad and *joyful*. They will have no sorrow or grief. (Isaiah 35:10)
- You don't see [Christ] now, but you believe in him. You are extremely *happy* with *joy* and praise. (1 Peter 1:8)

New English Translation

- You, O LORD, have made me *happy* by your work. I will sing for *joy* because of what you have done. (Psalm 92:4)
- Rejoice in the LORD and be *happy*, you who are godly! Shout for *joy*. (Psalm 32:11)
- Satisfy us in the morning with your loyal love! Then we will shout for *joy* and be *happy* all our days! (Psalm 90:14)

New Century Version

- Solomon sent the people home, full of *joy*. They were *happy* because the LORD had been so good. (2 Chronicles 7:10)
- [The believers] ate together in their homes, *happy* to share their food with *joyful* hearts. (Acts 2:46)

- If I have to offer my own blood with your sacrifice, I will be *happy* and full of *joy* with all of you. (Philippians 2:17)

Good News Translation

- Hannah prayed: "The LORD has filled my heart with *joy*; how *happy* I am because of what he has done!" (1 Samuel 2:1)
- When they saw [the star], how *happy* [the wise men] were, what *joy* was theirs! (Matthew 2:9-10)
- That day many sacrifices were offered, and the people were full of *joy* because God had made them very *happy*. (Nehemiah 12:43)

Is It True That Joy Isn't an Emotion?

A Christian writer says, "We don't get joy by seeking a better emotional life, because joy is not an emotion. It is a settled certainty that God is in control."[10] Another says, "Joy is not an emotion. It is a choice."[11]

The idea that "joy is not an emotion" (a statement that appears online more than 16,000 times) promotes an unbiblical concept.

A Bible study says, "Spiritual joy is not an emotion. It's a response to a Spirit-filled life."[12] But if this response doesn't involve emotions of happiness or gladness or delight or good cheer, in what sense is it "spiritual joy"?

Some claim that joy is a fruit of the Spirit and therefore not an emotion. But in Galatians 5:22, *love* and *peace* sandwich the word *joy*. If you love someone, don't you feel something for them? And what is peace if it doesn't involve feelings of contentment and satisfaction?

A hundred years ago, every Christian knew the meaning of joy. Today if you ask a group of Christians, "What is joy?" most will grope for words and come up with only one emphatic opinion: that joy is different from happiness—and superior to it.

Saying joy is without feelings is like saying rain isn't wet or ice isn't cold. Scripture, dictionaries, and common language—except the recent language of some churches— simply don't support this separation.

When God calls us to rejoice in him, does he care only about what we think and do, not how we *feel* about him? No. He commands us to love him not just with all our minds but with all our hearts (see Matthew 22:37).

Yes, it's possible to obey and serve God without feeling joy. But God rebukes those who do (see Deuteronomy 28:47-48). In other words, he emphatically says he *wants* us to feel joy!

The Father said twice, "This is my beloved Son, with whom I am well pleased" (Matthew 3:17; 17:5). To be well pleased means to feel pleasure. Whether you call those feelings joy, happiness, gladness, or delight—and

I think any and all are appropriate—the Father certainly felt them toward Jesus, and so should we.

When the Father said of his Son the Messiah, "Behold my servant, whom I uphold, my chosen, in whom my soul delights" (Isaiah 42:1), did he have feelings toward his Son? Have you ever delighted in someone without having strong feelings about that person? Weren't the Father's feelings toward his Son joyful?

The psalmist said, "I will go to the altar of God, to God my exceeding joy, and I will praise you with the lyre, O God, my God" (Psalm 43:4). Can you imagine saying to someone, "You are my exceeding joy," without feeling strong emotions toward them?

Reducing joy to an unemotional, otherworldly, purely "spiritual" state strips it of the delight God intended.

Throughout the 1987 movie *The Princess Bride*, the Sicilian mastermind Vizzini repeatedly uses the word *inconceivable* to describe event after event that actually happens. Finally, Inigo Montoya tells Vizzini, "You keep using that word. I do not think it means what you think it means."

His statement also applies to Christians who frequently use but often misunderstand the word *joy*. It doesn't mean what many people think it means.

The notion that we can have joy without happiness has perverted the meaning of both words and helped spawn a culture of Christian curmudgeons. Feeling morally superior, they may affirm that they have the joy of Jesus deep in their hearts, but apparently it's so deep it never makes its way to their faces. It never comes out in their words, either. Consider the number of "Christian" social media trolls who do nothing but look for opportunities to demean, criticize, and mercilessly judge motives.

Teaching seminary students about preaching, Charles Spurgeon said, "When you speak of heaven, let your face light up with a heavenly gleam. Let your eyes shine with reflected glory. And when you speak of hell—well, then your usual face will do."[13]

There's a Rich History of Equating Joy with Happiness

Puritan preacher Jonathan Edwards (1703–1758) cited John 15:11—Jesus' prayer that his "joy might remain in you" (KJV)—to prove this point: "The happiness Christ gives to his people, is a participation of his own happiness." This proves that joy and happiness were interchangeable to him. Edwards wrote of "the joy and happiness that the church shall have in her true bridegroom"[14] and spoke of believers as "these joyful happy persons."[15] Edwards used the words *joyful* and *happy* to reinforce, not contrast, each other.

Charles Spurgeon said, "May your Christian life be fraught with happiness, and overflowing with joy."[16]

Spurgeon's views of happiness and joy, evident in hundreds of his sermons, are completely contrary to the artificial wall the contemporary church has erected between joy and happiness.

With the help of Logos Bible software, I discovered that Spurgeon used *happiness* or *happy* more than 23,000 times in his sermons, the vast majority of them favorably.

Spurgeon routinely used *joy* and *happiness* interchangeably. He said, "A happy Christian attracts others by his joy."[17] Spurgeon described his conversion this way: "Oh, it was a joyful day, a blessed day! Happy day, happy day, when His choice was known to me, and fixed my choice on Him!"[18]

Spurgeon also declared, "Joy is a delightful thing. You cannot be too happy, Brothers and Sisters! No, do not suspect yourself of being wrong because you are full of delight. . . . Provided that it is joy in the Lord, you cannot have too much of it!"[19] Spurgeon gave that single qualification—"in the Lord"—when it comes to our happiness or joy. Happiness to Spurgeon was biblical and God honoring, not suspect or second class.

Spurgeon would have fully agreed with Mike Mason:

When I'm joyful, I'm happy, and when I'm happy, I'm joyful. What could be plainer? Why should I want anything to do with a

joy that isn't coupled with happiness, or
with a kind of happiness that is without joy?
Happiness without joy is shallow and transient
because it's based on outward circumstances
rather than an attitude of the heart. As for
joy without happiness, it's a spiritualized lie.
The Bible does not separate joy and happiness
and neither should we.[20]

We Need to Correct the Anti-Happiness Message

In the twentieth century, many Bible-believing churches moved from Spurgeon's "You cannot be too happy" to "God doesn't want you to be happy."

Some Christian leaders—Oswald Chambers was one among many—saw the word *happiness* applied to sinful activities (e.g., people abandoning their families to "be happy"), so they started speaking against happiness-seeking.

Their hatred of sin and disdain for pursuing it in the name of happiness was fully justified. But their response should have been, "God is happy and built us to desire happiness. He promises the highest form of happiness in Jesus. But we should seek happiness in him, never in sin." Sin, by the way, is never the friend of happiness; it is its ultimate enemy!

It's not too late to convey this message of Christ-centered happiness to our children and grandchildren and churches. Since they long for happiness, it's a message they desperately need to hear. Getting this message across requires both our words and our consistent example of living what the Bible calls the "good news of happiness."

I agree with Joni Eareckson Tada:

> We're often taught to be careful of the difference between joy and happiness. Happiness, it is said, is an emotion that depends upon what "happens." Joy by contrast, is supposed to be enduring, stemming deep from within our soul and which is not affected by the circumstances surrounding us. . . . I don't think God had any such hair-splitting in mind. Scripture uses the terms interchangeably along with words like delight, gladness, blessed. There is no scale of relative spiritual values applied to any of these.[21]

So what's the difference between what the Bible calls the "good news of happiness" (Isaiah 52:7) and the "good news of great joy" (Luke 2:10)? There is no difference. Both *happiness* and *joy* are great words. We need both of them, along with their synonyms, which include *pleasure*, *gladness*, *cheer*, and *merriment*. No one word is big enough to describe the sheer delight of who God is and what he has done for us in Jesus.

For too long we've distanced the gospel from what God created us to desire and what he desires for us—happiness.

We need to reverse the trend. Let's reclaim the word *happiness* in light of both Scripture and church history. Our message shouldn't be "Don't seek happiness" but "You'll find in Jesus the happiness you've always longed for."

CHAPTER 6

DOES "BLESSED" MEAN "HAPPY"?

GROWING UP IN an unbelieving home, I never heard the word *blessed* as a child. After I came to Christ, I heard it often. I didn't know what it meant; I just knew it sounded holy and spiritual. It was "white noise"—one of many undefined church words whose meanings are masked due to frequent use.

Years later, I heard someone say that in passages such as Psalm 1 and the Beatitudes of Matthew 5 and Luke 6, *blessed* actually means "happy." Because of what I'd read and been taught about God not wanting us to be happy, I was certain this must be wrong. I figured that someone was tinkering with God's Word and trying to superimpose the popular word *happy* on a Bible that has nothing to do with happiness.

If *blessed* meant "happy," I reasoned, why had no one told me that in the hundreds of books I'd already read? And if the Hebrew and Greek really meant "happy," why wasn't it translated that way in our Bibles? It made no sense.

Then I started digging for the truth. Many years later I dug deeper than ever while researching my book *Happiness*. My search yielded rich and surprising discoveries.

First, I found that there are more than twenty different Hebrew words and fifteen Greek words in Scripture that are synonyms for happiness. As I discuss in *Happiness*, the Bible doesn't merely include a few references to happiness, it is *full* of them![1]

Second, regarding the primary Hebrew and Greek words routinely translated *blessed*, I discovered that they do indeed mean something very different from what *blessed* meant to me.

Happiness Emerges in the Old Testament

To understand the happiness God offers his creatures, there's no word in Scripture more important than the Hebrew word *asher*.

If you have spent time with Bible reference books, you may know that *asher* means "happy" and that the

English word *blessed* used to translate it meant "happy" centuries ago.

Standard Hebrew dictionaries routinely give *happy* as the closest English equivalent for *asher*. Nevertheless, it's most commonly translated "blessed" instead.[2] Proverbs 28:14 is one of many examples of this: "Blessed is the one who always trembles before God" (NIV).

Commentaries and study notes explain that this verse means that the person who fears God is happy. But that thought would not even occur to most people when they see the word *blessed*. Of course, had *asher* been translated "happy" here—as it is more than twenty other times in the King James and most other English versions—the reader would immediately see the meaning without the need for commentaries or study notes.

If you played Password or Catch Phrase and the word was *happy*, you could figure it out if your partner gave you clues such as "joyful," "glad," "cheerful," and "delighted." But suppose someone offered you the clue "blessed." Would *happy* pop into your mind? More likely you'd respond to *blessed* by saying "fortunate" or "holy" or something else that's *not* a synonym for happy. And when you found out the key word was *happy*, you'd probably say, "Huh?" and wish for a different partner.

What Does the Word *Blessed* Mean Today?

There are millions of online references to the "Blessed Virgin Mary." Do most people suppose this means the "*Happy* Virgin Mary"? No. They would naturally think of the "Holy Virgin Mary." Likewise, upon hearing of "the blessed sacrament," few would think it means "the happy sacrament."

In the *Merriam-Webster Unabridged Dictionary*, the first synonym listed in the definition of *blessed* is "of, relating to, or being God."[3] The second definition is "set apart or worthy of veneration by association with God." The synonyms include "consecrate, consecrated, hallowed, sacral, sacred, sacrosanct, sanctified."

Every definition and synonym cited for *blessed* relates to holiness. Virtually nothing relates to happiness, though a few dictionaries acknowledge that it once meant "happy."

I asked people on my Facebook page, "What comes to mind when you hear the word *blessed*?" More than 1,100 responses followed. Some associated *blessed* with being covered, favored, or having peace and contentment. Others said that *blessed* means "lucky."

About 30 percent of responders mentioned "undeserved favor" from God, similar to the way most people would define *grace*.

Only 12 percent, roughly one out of nine people, made any mention of happiness, gladness, or joy.

Why Do English Translations Shy Away from the Word *Happy*?

Since the Hebrew word *asher* (as well as its complement in Greek, *makarios*) means "happy," then why isn't it consistently translated "happy"?

The simple answer is that when the King James Version translators rendered *asher* and *makarios* as "blessed," readers knew that *blessed* was a synonym for *happy*.

For several centuries after the KJV was translated, *blessedness* and *happiness* remained nearly interchangeable in common speech. This is evidenced by the 1828 edition of Noah Webster's dictionary, which defined *blessed* this way:

> Made happy or prosperous; extolled; pronounced happy. a. Happy; prosperous in worldly affairs; enjoying spiritual happiness and the favor of God; enjoying heavenly felicity.[4]

Likewise, it defined *blessedly* as "happily" and *blessedness* as "happiness."

This proves definitively that two hundred years ago, people still understood *blessed* to mean "happy." That's a striking contrast to the results of my poll about what *blessed* means today.

Without question, modern Bible translations would

not continue to render *asher* or *makarios* as "blessed" if not for the long history of respected English translations that do so.

My extensive research and dialogue with Hebrew and Greek scholars left me perplexed about why most translators continue to use the word *blessed* as a translation of *asher* and *makarios*.

Though it most often renders *makarios* as "blessed," the literally inclined New American Standard Bible translates Romans 14:22 as "Happy [*makarios*] is he who does not condemn himself in what he approves."

Why? William Tyndale (c. 1494–1536), a Reformer who translated the Bible into English in the sixteenth century, rendered *makarios* as "happy" in Romans 14:22, and the KJV followed Tyndale's example, as it usually did.

But if "happy" is a good translation of *makarios* here, then why isn't it translated the same way in the Beatitudes, where Jesus used it with exactly the same sentence construction: "*Makarios* are the merciful," etc.? Why do all the major English translations still say, "Blessed are" instead of "Happy are," despite the fact that to most people *blessed* no longer means "happy"?

The Beatitudes are a commonly known and memorized passage. Many people familiar with the traditional wording would balk at the change, feeling the Bible had been tampered with.

More than thirty years ago, my friend John R. Kohlenberger III, the author of dozens of Hebrew and Greek reference books, handed the newly updated New International Version to the religion editor of a major newspaper.

John told me that she immediately turned to the Beatitudes in Matthew 5 and was relieved to see that it said "blessed" rather than "happy." She told him she didn't like those modern translations that use "happy" instead of "blessed." So the revised NIV passed her test.

To this educated church woman, *blessed* sounded spiritual and *happy* sounded unspiritual. Familiarity was more important than accuracy.

Other Languages Translate *Blessed* as "Happy"

Experience has shown me that despite all the evidence, some people still push back on the idea that "happy" is the proper translation of *asher* and *makarios*. They resist the notion that God is called the "happy God" in 1 Timothy 1 and 6 and that the Beatitudes could be accurately rendered "Happy is the one who . . ."

If this is where you find yourself, perhaps it will be helpful to understand how non-English translations render these words in their own languages.

The United Bible Societies' New Testament Handbook Series is a twenty-volume set of linguistic insights used by translators worldwide. It helps them best render the New Testament into target languages, including those of people groups who don't have the Bible in their native languages.

For example, all the bestselling English Bible versions translate John 13:17 similar to the NIV: "Now that you know these things, you will be *blessed* if you do them" (emphasis added). But here's what the UBS handbook says about *makarios* in this verse:

> In the present passage, as in most other New Testament passages where this Greek word [*makarios*] occurs, the focus is upon the subjective state of happiness shared by persons who have received God's blessing. For this reason, the translation "happy" is preferable to "blessed."[5]

Dozens of similar comments in the UBS handbooks instruct translators worldwide to translate *makarios* with the closest equivalent to "happy" in their target language.

These guidelines have been followed for decades by innumerable translators. The result is that thousands of people groups all over the world know what relatively few English readers know—that the passages containing *makarios* (as well as its Old Testament Hebrew equivalent, *asher*) normally refer to being happy in God. (Wouldn't that be a great thing for English Bible readers to know too?)

Pascal, writing in his native French, used the word *heureux* when he said, "All men seek happiness." This word, found ninety-three times in Pascal's *Pensées*, is translated in every French-English dictionary as "happy." All four French translations of the Bible I found online use *heureux* to translate *makarios* in the Beatitudes. Hence, each line of Matthew 5:3-11 beginning with *heureux* shows French readers that Jesus offers the very happiness Pascal says all people seek.

Since *makarios* is translated as the equivalent of "happy" in French and thousands of other languages, shouldn't we expect the same in English? I find it remarkable that all of the top seven bestselling English translations usually translate *makarios* as "blessed," not "happy."

This means that English-speaking believers are uniquely vulnerable to the myth that most other Bible readers in the world are immune to: that the Bible says nothing about happiness and neither expects nor calls on us to be happy.

Is *Happy* a Dangerous Word?

I have heard people say it would be "dangerous" to translate *asher* and *makarios* as "happy," because doing so might "appeal to the flesh."

But wasn't it up to God which Hebrew and Greek words would be included in Scripture? If these terms are most accurately translated "happy," who are we to not do so? Isn't any Bible teacher capable of explaining that this happiness spoken of in Scripture cannot be found in sin but only in God?

Isn't it easy enough to balance the call to gladness in God by pointing out that this doesn't entail merely bubbly gleefulness but that we are to "weep with those who weep" (Romans 12:15) and that we can be "sorrowful, yet always rejoicing" (2 Corinthians 6:10)?

Speaking about Christ-centered happiness is fully compatible with pointing out the many passages demonstrating that prosperity theology is wrong, that often our life circumstances will be difficult, and that sorrow and grief are also part of the Christian life.

What's dangerous is not recognizing the happiness in God explicitly revealed in Scripture. What's dangerous is ignoring or denying it.

Other Words Have Cultural Baggage

Many good words are commonly misused and watered down. The word *holy* has lots of baggage too. To countless people, it means being self-righteous, intolerant, and out of touch with reality. Since people routinely misunderstand it, should we no longer use the word *holy*?

Likewise, *love* is commonly used in shallow ways, as popular music has long demonstrated. People say they love hamburgers, rock and roll, hairstyles, and YouTube. They "make love" to someone they barely know.

Since the word *love* has been so twisted and trivialized, should we remove it from Bible translations? Should we stop using the word in our families and churches?

Of course not. Instead, we should clarify what Scripture truly means by *love* and *holiness*, as well as terms like *hope*, *peace*, *pleasure*, and yes, *happiness*. When appropriate, we should contrast the meaning in Scripture with our culture's superficial and sometimes sinful connotations.

Why Does Translation Matter?

No unbeliever says, "What I most want in life is to be blessed." Nor is there danger of that familiar song being sung as "Blessed birthday to you."

The secularization of culture has shrunk the common vocabulary of believers and unbelievers. However, *happiness* is a word that should still convey rich meaning to both groups. Ironically, it's only some modern believers who devalue happiness while virtually no unbelievers do.

Wouldn't people be more attracted to the gospel if they were told about what Scripture reveals: a happy God and his offer of a deep, abiding happiness in Christ that begins now and goes on forever? I'm convinced they would.

As sinners, we are rebels against God—something we must come to terms with to embrace the gospel. Obviously the offer of happiness alone isn't the whole gospel and won't persuade rebels to change their allegiance. But since God himself calls the gospel "the good news of happiness," surely we should see happiness as a vital part of it.

Suppose an unbeliever who is struggling with depression and suicidal thoughts sees a display Bible open to Psalm 1 and reads, "Blessed is the one who . . ." Will that person feel a compulsion to read further? Probably not.

But suppose instead that person reads one of the dozen or more Bible translations that render *asher* not as "blessed" but as "happy." He or she would be introduced to God's Word this way: "How happy is the one who does not walk in the advice of the wicked or stand in the pathway with sinners or sit in the company of mockers!" (Psalm 1:1, CSB).

Do you see how this wording might reach someone who has gone down the wrong road, taken the wrong advice, searched in vain for happiness, and is now world weary?

If seekers read in the Beatitudes, "Happy are those who mourn, for they shall be comforted," they would probably be struck by the paradox. *Happiness and mourning at the same time? How is that even possible?*

That's what Jesus wanted his listeners to realize—he was offering them something counterintuitive, even miraculous, something God given that could never come from human invention or positive thinking.

Like every other word in Scripture, *asher* and *makarios* should be translated so readers understand the inspired, God-breathed meaning. The word *happiness* is central to the thinking and desires of unbelievers and believers alike. It's therefore a critically important bridge—one we should not burn. And if we have burned it—as I believe many modern Western churches have—let's do all we can to rebuild it!

We desperately need holiness, but it's happiness we long for. The church shouldn't retreat from such a significant word that was once central to the vocabulary of God's people. On the contrary, we should give happiness its proper biblical context, celebrate it, and embrace it as a vital part of the gospel message.

CHAPTER 7

WHERE DOES TRUE HAPPINESS BEGIN?

HUMAN HISTORY IS THE STORY of our desperate search for true and lasting happiness. Even those people who appear to "have it all" long for something more, and sadly, they often give up hope of ever finding contentment and joy.

In the midst of hopelessness, God offers the good news of his transforming grace, mercy, love, and eternal happiness: "Let the one who is thirsty come; let the one who wants it take the water of life free of charge" (Revelation 22:17, NET).

It's the Lord Who Truly Satisfies

Our greatest needs and longings can be fulfilled only in God, the "fountain of living waters" (Jeremiah 2:13).

Despairing people everywhere thirst for gladness, trying to derive it from sources that cannot ultimately satisfy. They eagerly drink from contaminated water surrounded by huge signs with neon letters flashing, "Fun and Happiness!"

Sometimes there's no fun at all, and usually what little happiness there is quickly evaporates, leaving shame and regret. If the signs were accurate, they would warn, "Deadly Poison," with the caveat underneath: "May taste good before it kills you."

God laments the poor choices we make when searching for happiness: "My people have committed two evils: they have forsaken me, the fountain of living waters, and hewed out cisterns for themselves, broken cisterns that can hold no water" (Jeremiah 2:13).

When we're thirsty, we don't look up "water" on Wikipedia. We don't go to social media to find out what others say about water. We don't drink out of the nearest puddle. Personally, I go to the faucet and satisfy my thirst by drinking some of the world's best water from the Bull Run water system here in Oregon.

Similarly, in the spiritual realm, I find God to be pure, refreshing, and satisfying. My happiest days are when I drink most deeply of him. I also know that if I don't drink of him, whatever else I drink from will leave me thirsty, dissatisfied, and sick.

George Whitefield wrote, "I drank of God's pleasure as out of a river. Oh that all were made partakers of this living water."[1]

Most Offers of Happiness Are Fraudulent

Jonestown was a socialist community and cult in South America. In 1978, after murdering a US congressman and four others, Jim Jones gathered his cult members, who had relocated from the United States to Guyana, and served them a grape-flavored drink laced with cyanide. He killed himself and 912 of his followers.

From this came the expression "Don't drink the Kool-Aid," which means, "Following someone blindly is a very bad idea." This is good advice for gullible people who are prone to believe that counterfeits can deliver happiness.

Trusting Jim Jones, and all fake sources of happiness, brings pain and loss. Jesus, in contrast, is fully worthy of our trust. He, who drank the cup of suffering on our behalf so we could be saved (see Matthew 26:27-28), makes this offer: "If anyone thirsts, let him come to me and drink. Whoever believes in me, as the Scripture has said, 'Out of his heart will flow rivers of living water'" (John 7:37-38).

We're free to be unhappy. We're free to search for happiness where it can't be found. We're free to eat chocolate-covered cyanide. What we're not free to do is reinvent

God, the universe, or ourselves so that what isn't from God will bring us happiness. It cannot, and it never will.

Are you thirsty for happiness—for meaning, peace, contentment? Jesus invites you to join hundreds of millions throughout history and across the globe, and a multitude of those now living in his immediate presence, to come to him and drink the best water in the universe—the only refreshment that will ever fully and eternally satisfy.

The Holy Spirit Delivers Happiness

Once we've come to Christ and experienced his refreshment, part of the Holy Spirit's ministry is to infuse us with happiness in God.

English theologian Richard Sibbes (1577–1635) wrote, "Though we have not always the joy of the Spirit, yet we have the Spirit of joy."[2] In other words, even in times of sorrow, happiness is not far away, since the Holy Spirit, who is also the Happy Spirit, indwells every believer.

Did you find it jarring to see the Holy Spirit referred to as the Happy Spirit? I am certainly not proposing a name change! But the Spirit's connection with happiness is explicitly biblical.

Nine qualities are listed as the fruit of the Spirit, the first being love and the second, joy (see Galatians 5:22-23). The Contemporary English Version renders it, "God's Spirit makes us loving, happy, peaceful, patient, kind . . ."

We're told that Kingdom living is "about pleasing God, about living in peace, and about true happiness. All this comes from the Holy Spirit" (Romans 14:17, CEV). Luke tells us that Jesus was "full of joy through the Holy Spirit" (Luke 10:21, NIV). The verse is also rendered this way: "The Holy Spirit made Jesus feel very happy" (ERV).

By being happy in the Holy Spirit, in Christ, and in the Father, we lay claim to the fact that God is infinitely bigger and more powerful than the Fall. We affirm that our Lord and Savior Jesus Christ will reverse the Curse and reign over a new universe.

By faith we draw upon that glorious and eternally happy world Christ purchased and promised us. Our present happiness whispers and sometimes shouts that our God lives among us and works in the world—and in our hearts—every minute of every hour of every day.

Can We Find Happiness in Nature?

Our happy God is the God of all beauty, which he kindly shares with all of us.

Thomas Traherne (1636–1674), an English poet and theologian, wrote, "Till you can sing and rejoice and delight in God . . . you never enjoy the world."[3]

Through God's kindness, unbelievers can experience limited joy, but when we know and love the

Creator—when we've tasted of his eternal refreshment—our heartfelt delight in his world is magnified. Seeking happiness in anything without God is like seeking water without wetness or sun without light.

When I was a young Christian, one of the hymns we often sang at my church featured these words:

> *Turn your eyes upon Jesus,*
> *Look full in his wonderful face,*
> *And the things of earth will grow strangely dim,*
> *In the light of his glory and grace.*[4]

If the things of Earth were all sinful, those words would make more sense. But shouldn't drawing close to our Creator make the beauties and wonders of his Earth brighter to us, not dimmer?

After coming to Christ, Jonathan Edwards said,

> The appearance of everything was altered; there seemed to be, as it were, a calm, sweet cast or appearance of divine glory in almost everything. God's excellency, his wisdom, his purity and love, seemed to appear in everything; in the sun, moon, and stars; in the clouds and blue sky; in the grass, flowers, trees; in the water and all nature.[5]

As I've walked with God over the decades, the sin-centered and shallow attractions of this Earth have indeed grown dimmer. But the happy-making beauties of this Earth's animals, trees, flowers, oceans, and sky, and of friends, family, good stories, great food, and music have grown brighter.

Finding our greatest pleasure in God elevates our enjoyment of those happiness-giving things. They're transformed from mud pies to mouthwatering desserts to be fully enjoyed—at the proper time and place—at the celebratory table of God's goodness.

Loving nature and beauty should be enhanced by loving the God who made them and reveals himself in them. How could it be otherwise?

Common Grace Is a Bridge to the Gospel

In a letter to his father, Scottish author George MacDonald (1824–1905) wrote of the barriers he faced in turning to Christ:

> One of my greatest difficulties in consenting
> to think of religion was that I thought I should
> have to give up my beautiful thoughts & my
> love for the things God has made. But I find that
> the happiness springing from all things not in
> themselves sinful is much increased by religion.

God is the God of the Beautiful, Religion the
Love of the Beautiful, & Heaven the House of
the Beautiful—nature is tenfold brighter in the
sun of righteousness, and my love of nature is
more intense since I became a Christian. . . .
God has not given me such thoughts, &
forbidden me to enjoy them. Will he not in
them enable me to raise the voice of praise?[6]

Paul built a bridge to the gospel through identifying
God as the universal source of happiness. Speaking to
unbelievers, Paul said that God "blessed you by giving you
rain from above as well as seasonal harvests, and satisfying
you with food and happiness" (Acts 14:17, CEB).

In the same context, Paul explained, "We are bringing
you good news, telling you to turn from these worthless
things to the living God, who made the heavens and the
earth and the sea and everything in them" (14:15, NIV).

Paul said that this same God who kindly gives us rain,
harvests, food, and happiness has done even more for
us—he has purchased eternal life for us in the redemptive work of Jesus!

Shouldn't we share this message today? Shouldn't we
say to people, "The same God who gives you food and
music and sports and pets and the wonders of creation
offers you eternal happiness in Jesus"?

This common grace from God extends to everyone. Jesus said that God "makes his sun rise on the evil and on the good, and sends rain on the just and on the unjust" (Matthew 5:45).

Living in Oregon, surrounded by stunning natural beauty, I often ponder the irony that according to a Gallup poll, Portland, Oregon, where Nanci and I and our children grew up, has by far the highest percentage of "religiously unaffiliated" people in the United States, with Seattle and San Francisco tied for second, nine percentage points behind.[7]

So if happiness comes from God, does this mean people who live in Portland can't sometimes be happy? No, because for the present, people can reject God while still enjoying the benefits of his common grace, including loving relationships; natural and artistic beauty; and physical, emotional, and intellectual pleasure.

The bad news is that those who deny God are living on borrowed time. This temporary situation will come to an abrupt end (see Hebrews 9:27-28; Revelation 20:11-15). David Murray identifies six kinds of happiness available to unbelievers and believers alike:

- nature happiness
- social happiness
- vocational happiness

- physical happiness
- intellectual happiness
- humor happiness

The one remaining component, available only to believers, is spiritual happiness. Murray calls this "a joy that at times contains more pleasure and delight than the other six put together."[8]

Spiritual happiness comes in contemplating God and drawing close to him. Of course, the other six aren't "unspiritual" forms of happiness. Because they're God given, they're spiritual, though not redemptive. But without the seventh kind of happiness, the first six are temporary.

After the termination of this present life, we can have one of two combinations:

- both God and happiness
- neither God nor happiness

What we will never have again is God without happiness or happiness without God.

Holiness Isn't Enough

The simple truth is that we seek not what actually will make us happy but whatever we *think* will make us happy.

A teenage boy came to me with questions about his

faith. He'd attended church all his life but now had some doubts. I assured him that even the writers of the Bible sometimes struggled. He wasn't questioning any basic Christian beliefs, so I talked to him about holiness and happiness.

"What does God's holiness mean?" I asked.

He gave a clear, biblical answer: "He's perfect, without sin."

"Absolutely true. Does thinking about God's holiness draw you to him?"

He responded sadly, "No."

I asked him whether he wanted to be holy 100 percent of the time.

"No."

"Me neither," I said. "I should, but I don't."

Then I surprised him by asking, "What do you want 100 percent of the time?"

He didn't know the answer.

"Have you ever once thought, *I don't want to be happy*?"

"No."

"Isn't that what you really want—happiness?"

He nodded, his expression saying, *Guilty as charged.* Friendships, sports, academics, video games—every activity, every relationship he chose—played into his desire to be happy. But I could see he felt that this longing was unspiritual, displeasing to God.

I opened the Bible and told him the word translated "blessed" in 1 Timothy 1:11 and 6:15 speaks of God being happy. I asked him to memorize these verses, replacing "blessed God" with "happy God."

Then I asked him to list as many things as he could think of that pointed him to God's happiness. They included backpacking, music, playing hockey, and favorite foods.

I said, "God could have made food without flavor, but he's a happy God, so he created a world full of happiness. That means you can thank him for macaroni and cheese, for music, for Ping-Pong, and above all, for dying on the cross so you can know him and be forever happy."

This young man had seen Christianity as a long list of things he should do that he didn't think would make him happy and an even longer list of things he shouldn't do that he imagined would have made him happy. That is a toxic faith—a faith that absolutely will not survive.

There's Far Better News

Whether we realize it or not, we'll choose the life we believe will make us happy. We'll live a wealth-centered life if we believe wealth brings happiness. We'll live a God-centered life if we believe God brings happiness. Just as no one shops for milk at a junkyard, no one seeks happiness from a cranky God. We never go to anyone to get what we don't believe they have.

In the movie *Chariots of Fire*, Olympic hopeful and eventual gold medalist Eric Liddell is challenged by his sister, Jennie, about his decision to train for the Olympics. He plans to leave for the mission field but delays so he can attempt to qualify in the 400-meter race. In doing so, Jennie thinks he's putting God second. (At least that's how she's portrayed in the movie, which appears in reality to have been unfair to her.[9]) But Eric sees things differently. He explains, "God . . . made me fast, and when I run, I feel his pleasure."[10]

The movie's version of Eric and Jennie shows two people who believe in the same God . . . yet don't. Both of them fear and love God. Both are committed to serving Christ. But Eric, who smiles warmly and signs autographs while his sister looks on disapprovingly, has something she lacks: a relaxed, heartfelt awareness of God's happiness—in his creation, in his people, and in all of life, including sports and competition.

Eric wants to serve God as much as his sister does, but he senses God's delight and purpose in making him a fast runner. If God finds pleasure in the majesty of a horse (see Job 39:19-25), surely he finds even greater pleasure in Eric's running for the pure joy of it. Because of the God-centered joy this gift brings him, Eric tells

Jennie that giving up running "would be to hold [God] in contempt."[11]

Both Eric and his sister want to reach the world with the gospel. But Eric's good news is far better news. Why? Because it's about more than deliverance from Hell—he understands that God is delightfully engaged in *all* he has created, not just church and ministry. In the eyes of both believers and unbelievers, Eric Liddell's belief in a happy God makes his life profoundly attractive.

CHAPTER 8

WHAT KILLS OUR HAPPINESS?

THE HAPPY LIFE IS to worship God as God—not putting anything or anyone else in his place. But in this fallen world, we can't simply affirm God as the source of happiness without dealing with the competition.

Idols Claim to Offer Happiness

Potential idols can be legitimate sources of happiness when enjoyed in their proper place. However, they become contaminated when we elevate them above the only true God. In other words, happiness becomes idolatrous when we try to find happiness apart from our Creator and Redeemer.

In the first two chapters of Genesis, God had no competition for the affection of his creatures. Humanity found its meaning, purpose, and happiness in God. God was God; everything else wasn't. And the only two humans knew it.

The Fall tragically changed that. Ever since, every member of the human race has been an idolater. What began in Eden won't end until Jesus returns and all idols crumble under his feet.

We Look for Happiness in All the Wrong Places

Despite the fact that we're surrounded by shows such as *American Idol* and the adulation of movie stars, musicians, and professional athletes, most twenty-first-century Americans don't believe we're a nation of idol worshipers. The word *idol* conjures up images of primitive people offering sacrifices to crude carved images. Surely we're above that.

Or are we?

An idol is *anything* we praise, celebrate, fixate on, and look to for help that's not the true God. That covers a lot of ground.

What are some of the idols people worship in our culture today? This list might surprise you:

- loving family relationships
- supportive friendships

- intellectual advancement, education, and learning
- reputation, popularity, and fame
- meaningful work
- serving others
- self-expression (artistic, musical, literary, etc.)
- leisure, hobbies, and entertainment
- sports
- politics, power, influence, and success
- leaving a legacy
- faith, spirituality, religion, and philosophy
- health and fitness
- beauty and youthfulness
- comfort
- food and drink
- sex
- wealth

In *Counterfeit Gods*, Tim Keller writes,

Each culture is dominated by its own set of
idols. . . . We may not physically kneel before
the statue of Aphrodite, but many young women
today are driven into depression and eating
disorders by an obsessive concern over their body
image. We may not actually burn incense to
Artemis, but when money and career are raised

to cosmic proportions, we perform a kind of
child sacrifice, neglecting family and community
to achieve a higher place in business and gain
more wealth and prestige.[1]

Idols often trap us not with obvious evils but by twisting what's good.

C. S. Lewis (1898–1963) portrayed this conversation
between two demons talking about God:

> He's a hedonist at heart. All those fasts and vigils
> and stakes and crosses are only a façade. Or
> only like foam on the seashore. Out at sea, out
> in His sea, there is pleasure, and more pleasure.
> He makes no secret of it; at His right hand are
> "pleasures for evermore." Ugh! . . . There are
> things for humans to do all day long without
> His minding in the least—sleeping, washing,
> eating, drinking, making love, playing, praying,
> working. Everything has to be *twisted* before it's
> any use to us.[2]

Lewis pointed out a great irony, one we shouldn't miss:
since the devil can't create, he has only God's good creation to use as temptations. Hence, he must twist what
God made in order to serve his evil purposes. He never

acts for our good, since he hates us just as he hates God, who made us in his likeness.

When the fulfillment of a desire is seen as a gift and is gratefully enjoyed for God's glory, we find satisfying happiness. When it's not, we become miserable, enslaved to the very thing that was intended by God as a loving gift.

Idolatry isn't just wrong—it fails miserably in bringing the lasting happiness it promises.

What Should We Do with Our Idols?

We must remove from the throne of our hearts every false god, both for God's glory and our good.

Scripture speaks strongly about the sin of idolatry: "Woe to those who go down to Egypt for help, and rely on horses, who trust in chariots because they are many, and in horsemen because they are very strong, but who do not look to the Holy One of Israel, nor seek the LORD!" (Isaiah 31:1, NKJV).

God calls us to ruthlessly dethrone false gods: "This is what you are to do to them: Break down their altars, smash their sacred stones, cut down their Asherah poles and burn their idols in the fire" (Deuteronomy 7:5, NIV).

John Piper says, "We all make a god out of what we take the most pleasure in."[3] The one way to avoid idolatry is to take the most pleasure in the one true God.

As Christ-followers, we shouldn't be more tolerant of

our idols than God was of Israel's. Once we recognize those idols, we can destroy them, exalting God alone. Only then can we know lasting happiness, for all lesser pleasures are only shadows of the real thing.

Let's take a closer look at a few of those idols that tempt us to trust in them instead of in the true God.

Health and Wealth Can Be Idols

I will focus on the idols of health and wealth together because among Christians they are often joined as dual idols in what's called "prosperity theology." What we'll learn here carries over to nearly every other good thing we can idolize.

Obviously it's not unspiritual to desire health over sickness, wealth over poverty, and success over failure. But if the ultimate source of our happiness isn't God, then health, wealth, and success become idols. God becomes a mere means to the end of what we *really* want. That end cannot be sustained—your life may not be long, but even if it is, your health *will* eventually fail. There have been no exceptions to that rule in all human history. (Even though Lazarus was raised from the dead, eventually he died again.)

Prosperity theology teaches that God will bless with material abundance and good health those who obey him and lay claim to his promises. "We don't have to wait for

God's blessing in the life to come," this ideology claims. "He'll send it to us here and now."

I don't want to be uncharitable, but I will be blunt: I believe that prosperity theology, with its practice of twisting some Scriptures while ignoring others, is straight from the pit of Hell. Centered on telling people they deserve whatever they want, this worldview treats God as a cosmic slot machine: insert a positive confession, pull the lever, catch the winnings.

In prosperity theology, "faith" becomes a crowbar to break down the door of God's reluctance rather than a humble attempt to access his willingness. Sadly, claiming that God must take away an illness or a financial hardship often means calling on him to remove the very things he has permitted and designed to make us more Christlike.

No matter how much we may appear to trust God and his promises, clinging to the American dream of health and wealth is idolatrous.

The Apostle Paul Didn't Have Health and Wealth

Jesus said of himself, "The Son of Man has no place to lay his head" (Matthew 8:20). He owned very little, and he promised his disciples, "In this world you will have trouble" (John 16:33, NIV).

Paul, the last apostle Jesus called, said, "To keep me from becoming conceited because of the surpassing greatness of the revelations, a thorn was given me in the flesh" (2 Corinthians 12:7). We don't know exactly what Paul's thorn in the flesh was, but it was most likely some kind of sickness or disability.

Paul recognized God had a purpose in it, to protect him from pride. Then Paul went right on to call that same adversity "a messenger of Satan, to torment me." Two supernatural beings, adamantly opposed to each other, are said in a single verse to have distinct purposes in sending Paul a disability.

God's purpose for Paul was to keep his eyes on him; Satan's purpose was to torment him and turn him from God.

Paul said he asked God three times to heal him, but God chose not to. This is proof that the prayers of godly people are not always answered. God did, however, reveal what he wanted Paul to learn by not answering his prayers: "My grace is sufficient for you, for my power is made perfect in weakness" (2 Corinthians 12:9).

Paul's thorn was a daily reminder of his need to trust in God's grace rather than his own gifts. When God chose not to heal him, Paul didn't "name it and claim it." Instead, he acknowledged God's spiritual purposes in his adversity.

Prosperity Theology Has Consequences

When health is our idol, and when we believe God must always heal us, then sickness will rob us of happiness in God.

Not only was Paul himself not healed from his thorn in the flesh, he also left Trophimus sick in Miletus (see 2 Timothy 4:20). His beloved friend Epaphroditus was gravely ill (see Philippians 2:24-30). Timothy, his son in the faith, had frequent stomach disorders. Paul didn't tell Timothy to claim healing—instead, he told him to drink a little wine to help his stomach (see 1 Timothy 5:23).

Ever since Nero had him beheaded nearly two thousand years ago, Paul has been enjoying perfect health and untold wealth. Still, like many of God's servants, while Paul was on Earth, God's plan was for him to often lack both health and wealth.

But because Paul trusted God, not his health or his wealth or anything else, in the midst of adversity, Paul was able to say, "Be happy in your faith at all times. Never stop praying. Be thankful, whatever the circumstances may be" (1 Thessalonians 5:16-18, PHILLIPS).

There's an important difference between the happy-sounding health-and-wealth mentality and true Christ-centered happiness. The primary source of our happiness isn't our circumstances but God, who promised to be with us always and who both commands and invites us to delight in him.

Sometimes We Need to Lose Our Faith

While we should never lose our faith in God, we often need to lose our faith in what isn't God.

Unlike today's jewelry-draped televangelists, Paul said, "We must go through many hardships to enter the kingdom of God" (Acts 14:22, NIV). Paul says we should not be "unsettled by these trials. For you know quite well that we are destined for them" (1 Thessalonians 3:3, NIV). This teaching could not be any more contradictory of prosperity theology.

As Nanci and I have spent the last eight months dealing with treatments for her cancer, it has encouraged us to know God has sovereignly sent this trial to us and is lovingly using it to make us more like Jesus. When righteous Job lost everything, even his children, he worshiped God, saying, "The LORD gave and the LORD has taken away; may the name of the LORD be praised" (Job 1:21, NIV). We're told, "In all this, Job did not sin by charging God with wrongdoing" (verse 22, NIV).

In contrast, when advocates of the prosperity gospel lose their health and wealth, they lose their happiness, demonstrating that the true object of their faith was never

God. Many, in fact, don't have faith in God; they have faith in their faith.

True faith doesn't insist that we say, "I'll conquer this cancer." Rather, we can affirm, "I know God can heal me, and I'll ask him to do so, and I'll do my best to get well. But I trust him. I pray he'll accomplish his best whether through healing and ongoing life or through sickness and death."

Some will write off this kind of prayer as faithless since it acknowledges the possibility of death. But aside from the return of Christ in our lifetimes, which is possible but far from certain, *we will all certainly die.* (Seriously, do you know any 120-year-old faith healers?)

Our prayers should be earnest, unapologetic requests for what we desire, uttered in willing submission to whatever our sovereign and loving God knows to be best.

There's an Antidote to Prosperity Theology

What we need is not faith in the idol of prosperity theology, but faith in the true God of the Bible.

A life focused on God allows us to rejoice in whatever health and wealth he entrusts to us as stewards but reminds us that he never promises these as permanent conditions in the present fallen world.

Some Christians are called upon to sacrifice their health through long hours of labor or by enduring persecution. We should be willing to lay everything on the line for Jesus because our life focus is on God, not self, health, or wealth—and not happiness either, in any form other than happiness in God, which is his command and calling.

A man showed me a note written by his fellow Iranian Christ-follower who had been imprisoned and separated from his family for three years. He wrote, "They say I'm the happiest man in this prison, and I believe they're right."

If our happiness is grounded in God, like this man's is, we'll never lose the basis for it. Why? Because nothing can separate us from the love of Christ (see Romans 8:37-39).

The gladness of God's children isn't the pasted-on, fake-it-till-you-make-it posturing of the prosperity gospel. Rather, it's the deep and resonant happiness of those who know and trust the Lord of the true gospel—the God with the nail-scarred hands.

CHAPTER 9

IS IT OKAY TO FIND HAPPINESS IN GOD'S GIFTS?

As we saw in the previous chapter, we must be careful not to make idols out of God's provisions. But God is happy when, with proper perspective, we fully enjoy his gifts to us. The key is to look to him as the ultimate source and provider and to thank and praise him for his kindness.

When we enjoy a delicious meal or a fun event, God isn't in Heaven frowning at us, saying, "Stop it—you should find joy only in me." This would be as foreign to our heavenly Father's nature as it would be to mine as an earthly father if I gave my daughters or grandchildren Christmas gifts and then got angry or pouted because they enjoyed them too much.

Jesus said, "If you then, who are evil, know how to give good gifts to your children, how much more will your Father who is in heaven give good things to those who ask him!" (Matthew 7:11).

Yes, God wants us to find our primary joy in him. But a large part of our happiness comes when we find joy in—and praise him for—his gifts to us.

Should We Seek the Giver, Not the Gift?

The idea that we should seek the giver, not the gift, has truth behind it, but it can be misleading.

Suppose I said to my wife, "Nanci, I love you. Therefore I will not love the meals you cook, the books you gave me, the Christmas presents from you, or the vacation we went on."

Would that make any sense? No. If I love gifts and vacation more than I love Nanci, that would obviously be wrong. But as long as she is foremost in my mind, by loving the meal Nanci prepares and the books she gives me, I honor her. So it is with God.

I can appreciate and enjoy a bike ride on a beautiful day, fully aware that the pure pleasure of it is God's gift to me. By enjoying it, I'm enjoying *him*.

Many believers have overspiritualized church, preaching, and prayer, and in doing so they have distanced God from creation, pleasure, and happiness. "Seek the giver, not the gift" can be an apt warning against idolatry in certain contexts, but as a general rule, it's misguided.

What we should say instead is, "Seek the giver *through* the gift" or "*in* the gift." Nanci and I are right to thoroughly enjoy the wonderful meals we have with four close friends on Thursday nights. We're aware that our friends and the food, and our capacity to enjoy both, are God's gifts to us. By enjoying these gatherings, in which we often speak of him, we are enjoying our Lord.

French Reformer John Calvin (1509–1564) wrote, "In despising the gifts, we insult the Giver."[1]

Scripture commands us to "earnestly desire the greater gifts" (1 Corinthians 12:31, NIV). But desiring God's gifts does not mean we must value the gifts above him.

Dissociating God from his gifts isn't the solution; it's the problem. Instead of viewing God's gifts as demonic temptations, we should view them as benevolent extensions of his love and grace. His gifts to us are not gods—but they are God's.

As long as we see God in his gifts to us, we need not be suspicious of them. We need not feel shame because they make us happy—they are simply doing what he designed them to do.

God is the primary source of all happiness. He has filled the world with secondary sources of happiness.

They are all tributaries that can be traced back to the roaring rivers and boundless oceans of God's own happiness that he will reveal for his children throughout eternity (see Ephesians 2:7).

God himself is by far the greatest gift. As long as we see God in his gifts to us and thank him wholeheartedly for them, we need not fear we're appreciating them too much.

God Wants Us to Enjoy His Creation

We are made in God's image, which includes a capacity to enjoy God's handiwork. Scripture tells us, "God saw everything that he had made, and behold, it was very good" (Genesis 1:31). Another version says his creation was "supremely good" (CEB).

A. W. Tozer beautifully depicted the happiness of God as seen in his creation:

> God is not only pleased with Himself, delighted
> with His own perfection and happy in His
> work of creating and redeeming, but He is
> also enthusiastic. There is an enthusiasm in
> the Godhead, and there is enthusiasm in
> creation. . . . This infinite God is enjoying
> Himself. Somebody is having a good
> time in heaven and earth and sea and sky.

Somebody is painting the sky. Somebody
is making trees to grow . . . causing the
ice to melt . . . and the fish to swim and
the birds to sing. . . . Somebody's running
the universe.[2]

The world around us brims with evidence of God's desire, and hence his provision, for his creatures' happiness.

Psalms 8, 19, and 139 are just a few of the many Scriptures that celebrate the wonders of God in his creation.

All creation is to celebrate its God: "Let the heavens rejoice, let the earth be glad. . . . Let the sea resound, and all that is in it; let the fields be jubilant, and everything in them!" (1 Chronicles 16:31-32, NIV).

Job said,

Ask the animals, and they will teach you, or the
birds in the sky, and they will tell you; or speak
to the earth, and it will teach you, or let the fish
in the sea inform you. Which of all these does
not know that the hand of the LORD has done
this? In his hand is the life of every creature and
the breath of all mankind.

JOB 12:7-10, NIV

It's right to find beauty, wonder, and happiness not only in God's natural creation but in the cultural gifts he's lavished upon his image bearers, including language, art, music, literature, drama, sports, careers, and hobbies, which allow us to be subcreators. These things generate no light of their own. The light they bring comes from "the Father of lights, with whom there is no variation or shadow" (James 1:17).

I don't value the planets and the moon less because they don't shine by their own light. Likewise, I don't devalue my wife, children, grandchildren, coworkers, or dog because they're secondary to God. On the contrary, I value them more, because the God who is primary has made them who and what they are, and he has endowed them with value that makes them far more important than if they were merely random accidents.

Consider this fatherly advice given in an ancient culture without refined sugar, in which nature's greatest treat was honey: "My son, eat honey, for it is good, and the drippings of the honeycomb are sweet to your taste" (Proverbs 24:13).

The father doesn't warn his son to stay away from honey because he might love honey more than God. If you know where honey comes from (it's not just from bees), to be happy with honey is to be happy with God. People's happiness with God's abundant gifts makes God happy too.

Are Our Bodies Inferior to Our Spirits?

Scripture doesn't view body and spirit as adversaries, since God created both and redeems both.

There are times when, as Jesus said, "the spirit indeed is willing, but the flesh is weak" (Matthew 26:41). Yet our bodies aren't prisons. They're an essential and God-designed aspect of our beings, meant to disclose our Creator.

We're not just spirits who occupy bodies the way hermit crabs inhabit a seashell. We are *spirit and body joined together by God*. Your body does not merely house the real you—it is as much a part of who you are as your spirit is. That's why the resurrection is essential to our glorification, which will involve the restoration of our full humanity.

God made the material world not to hinder our walk with him but to facilitate it.

Tragically, though, some Christians are wary of physical beauties and pleasures because of an unbiblical belief that the spirit realm is good while the material world is bad. I call this *Christoplatonism*, a term I coined in my book *Heaven*.[3] It's a widespread belief, plaguing countless Christians and churches over the years, convincing people that physical pleasures are unspiritual and therefore many of the things that make people happy are suspect and even sinful.

The anti-body, anti-Earth, anti-culture assumptions of Christoplatonism naturally lend themselves to an anti-happiness viewpoint. Instead of seeing spiritual as the opposite of ungodly, many Christians see it as the opposite of physical and pleasurable. Such people oppose happiness and pleasure even in their most innocent forms.

In contrast, David rejoiced in good food and drink: "You prepare a feast for me in the presence of my enemies. . . . My cup overflows with blessings" (Psalm 23:5, NLT).

Why did God give us the ability to find joy in going for a cool swim, taking a hot shower, listening to music, reading stories, eating pistachios, planting flowers, or running through a park? Why did he give us physical senses if not to know him better and to be far happier in him than we ever could be if he had instead made us disembodied spirits?

It's no coincidence that the apostle Paul's detailed defense of the physical resurrection was written to the church at Corinth. Corinthian believers were immersed in the Greek philosophies of Platonism and dualism, which perceived a dichotomy between the spiritual and physical realms.

Platonists see a disembodied soul as the ideal. The Bible, meanwhile, views this division as unnatural and undesirable. We are unified beings. That's why Paul said that if there is no resurrection, "we are of all people most to be pitied" (1 Corinthians 15:19).

Creation Should Delight Us

Some Christians' anti-physical worldview causes them to envision the eternal Heaven as a place where spirits exist in a "higher plane" of disembodied angelic spirituality.

This misguided perspective that bodies, Earth, material things, and anything "secular" are automatically unspiritual negates the emphatic biblical revelation about bodily resurrection and finding joy in God's physical creation. We are told to look forward to the New Heaven and New Earth, which will be nothing less than a remade physical universe (see 2 Peter 3:13).

Any views of the afterlife that settle for less than a full bodily resurrection—including Christoplatonism, reincarnation, and transmigration of the soul—are explicitly anti-Christian. The early church waged doctrinal wars against heresies that contradict the biblical account, where God calls all creation "very good" (Genesis 1:31).

The movie *Babette's Feast* depicts a conservative Christian sect that scrupulously avoids "worldly" distractions. They live out the unhappy philosophy of Christoplatonism—quick to judge, slow to rejoice, and convinced that celebration, pleasure, and laughter must be sinful.

Then Babette, once a gourmet cook in France, is forced by war to become a maid for the two women who lead this small group of austere believers. Babette unexpectedly inherits a significant sum of money and, out of gratitude for their kindness to her, spends it all to prepare a fabulous dinner party for the elderly sisters and their friends.

Touched by Babette's generosity and the great feast she prepared, the community's false guilt dissipates, and they begin to laugh, take delight, and truly enjoy the richness of God's provision. Over the many courses of this meal, these legalists gradually come to understand that when God and his gifts are the objects of our happiness, feasting and laughter and beauty draw us not away from God but to him.[4]

How sad when the world doesn't see God as the source of creation's goodness. And how much sadder still when God's people don't see it.

Feasting Is a Great Thing

Singing, dancing, feasts, and festivities depict not only worship but delight in God's good gifts.

Proverbs 15:15 says, "The cheerful of heart has a continual feast." A feast is the ultimate picture of happiness—and for the Jewish people, the Sabbath meant there was at least one feast per week. In addition, there were a number of weeklong festivals that ensured people would eat together.

Words describing eating, meals, and food appear more

than a thousand times in Scripture, with the English translation "feast" occurring an additional 187 times. Feasting is profoundly relational, marked by conversation, storytelling, and laughter. Biblical feasts were spiritual gatherings that drew attention to God, his greatness, and his redemptive purposes.

Of course, God forbids drunkenness and gluttony (two sins that ultimately make us not only unholy but also unhappy). But the partying described repeatedly in Scripture reveals the happiness of the God who invented feasts and festivals and who commands and encourages singing, dancing, eating, and drinking.

The people of Israel found happiness in God's feasts. By building multiple festivities into Israel's calendar, God integrated joy into the lives of his people. These feast days served to link happiness with holiness. Festivals such as the Feast of Tabernacles included sacrifices for sin (see Leviticus 23:37-41). Sorrow over sin and its redemptive price was real but momentary. Once the sacrifices were complete, the festival became all about enjoying God and one another.

Feasts that recognized repentance, forgiveness, and redemption included more joy than any party pagans could host, because the participants' delight was deep, God centered, and based in reality.

"Happy are those whose transgression is forgiven,

whose sin is covered" (Psalm 32:1, NRSV). In light of such good news, who wouldn't want to celebrate? And why shouldn't we, who know the grace of Jesus, do the same, since the gospel gives us even *more* reasons to celebrate?

The church father Chrysostom (347–407) said, "All life is a festival since the Son of God has redeemed you from death."[5]

Jesus repeatedly mentioned to his disciples that after we're resurrected, we'll eat together, enjoying the company of familiar biblical figures. He said, "Many will come from east and west and recline at table with Abraham, Isaac, and Jacob in the kingdom of heaven" (Matthew 8:11). This must have delighted his listeners. It should delight us, too!

What If We Viewed Church as a Party Scene?

Wouldn't it be great if the church were known for celebrating *more* than the world does, rather than less? After all, don't we have far more to celebrate?

Worship, camaraderie, and unity would be hallmarks of such celebratory events. But one of the greatest payoffs would be reestablishing followers of Jesus as people of profound happiness, quick to celebrate the greatness, goodness, love, grace, and happiness of our God.

In today's worship settings, "fellowship" may involve moderate laughter, but rarely does it reflect the great happiness the Bible describes. Indeed, the difference between the grand feast of the Lord's Supper in the New Testament and the symbolic wafers and grape juice offered by most modern churches at Communion is the difference between a great celebration on the one hand and a minimalist ritual on the other.

Spurgeon said this about the most sacred rituals of the church, particularly Communion: "Gospel ordinances are choice enjoyments, enjoined upon us by the loving rule of Him whom we call Master and Lord. We accept them with joy and delight. . . . The Lord's own Supper is a joyful festival, a feast."[6]

God's people ought to say, "Let us eat, drink, and be merry today to celebrate the time when we'll eat, drink, and be merry in a world without suffering and without end!"

Were we to do more of this kind of celebrating, and do it better, surely fewer of our children (and generations to come) would fall for what may be the enemy's deadliest and most effective lie—that the gospel of Jesus doesn't offer happiness and that people must go elsewhere to find it.

CHAPTER 10

WHAT KEY UNLOCKS
HAPPINESS?

"WHAT IS THE MATTER with the world?" asked Welsh minister Martyn Lloyd-Jones (1899–1981). "Why . . . war and all this unhappiness and turmoil and discord amongst men? . . . There is only one answer to these questions— sin. Nothing else; it is just sin."[1]

We commonly blame the world's suffering and unhappiness on lack of education or resources. *If only we knew more or had more, everything would be fixed.*

No.

Our most basic problem is just . . . sin. First our own, then the rest of the world's.

Puritan clergyman Stephen Charnock (1628–1680) wrote, "Though the fall be the cause of all our misery, yet [recognizing] it is the first step to all our happiness."[2]

There are paradoxical truths surrounding sin and forgiveness. On the one hand, these things are true of those who have put their faith in Jesus:

- There is therefore now no condemnation for those who are in Christ Jesus. (Romans 8:1)
- As far as the east is from the west, so far has he removed our transgressions from us. (Psalm 103:12, NIV)

On the other hand, though we are forgiven of our past sins, including some we don't remember, we are called upon to confess our sins as we become aware of them: "If we confess our sins, he is faithful and just to forgive us our sins and to cleanse us from all unrighteousness" (1 John 1:9).

It may seem confusing that we must continue to confess recent sins in order to experience new and fresh forgiveness. But while we have a settled once-and-for-all forgiveness in Christ, we also have a current ongoing relationship with him that is hampered by unconfessed sin.

While the Prodigal Son was fully forgiven and welcomed home by his father, when he sinned against him a week later, he needed to acknowledge that offense also in order to keep the relationship clean and strong.

The good news is that it's easier to be restored to a

positive relationship with God than with any other being. As difficult as this is to grasp, when we do, it's happy-making in the extreme.

God is the holiest being in the universe, meaning that his standards are infinitely higher than any creature's. It would be easy to conclude, then, that God would be more prone than anyone else to hold our offenses against us. Yet the opposite is true. Who else will forgive us of everything, absolutely and always?

It's not the sinless God but sinful people who sometimes refuse to forgive. Nothing we've done or ever will do can surprise God or cause him to change his mind about us. No skeletons will fall out of our closets in eternity. He has seen us at our worst, and he still loves us. Arms wide open, he invites our confession and repentance, which he always meets with his grace and forgiveness.

How secure are we in God's love? Jesus said, "My sheep hear my voice, and I know them, and they follow me. I give them eternal life, and they will never perish, and no one will snatch them out of my hand" (John 10:27-28). True happiness can come only in realizing sin, admitting it, and seeking the only solution—the forgiveness of Jesus based on his redemptive work. In forgiveness alone we can have relational oneness with God and, hence, enduring happiness.

Satan Lies about Happiness

The devil hates God's happiness and ours.

Satan forfeited forever his own happiness, and he bitterly hates us—the objects of God's love. Since he's committed to making us just as miserable as he is, the devil tempts us toward what will dishonor God.

His lies convince us we'll find happiness in things that ultimately make us miserable. After doing this for thousands of years, he's remarkably good at this deception. Jesus said of Satan, "When he lies, he speaks his native language, for he is a liar and the father of lies" (John 8:44, NIV).

The devil specializes in catching us on the baited hook of pleasure. The first hit of a drug or the thrill of illicit sex seems so good in the moment. Then the very thing that brings us a taste of joy rots in our mouths and robs us of true and abiding joy. Sin is the ultimate killjoy.

To sin is to break relationship with God. Since our connection to God is our connection to happiness, sin is the biggest enemy of happiness. And that makes forgiveness its greatest friend. Confession reunites us with the one from whom happiness flows. No wonder Satan relentlessly tries to enslave us to sin, then urges us to deny sin and refuse to recognize and confess it.

Since God is the source of happiness and the creator of our capacity and desire for happiness, and Satan is the greatest hater of happiness in the universe, Christians who spend their lives sourly sniffing out happiness and trying to squelch it should ask themselves, *Whose side am I on?*

Feelings of Guilt Can Be Good

Confession changes everything—for the better.

I received an e-mail from a young man in college who had engaged in immorality. His despair was palpable. Of course, an unbeliever might suppose his misery was due to unnecessary guilt feelings. But in this case, these feelings were accurate indicators of genuine guilt.

This young man might feel temporarily happier if he denied his guilt. Likewise, someone jumping from a plane, not realizing his parachute is defective, can be temporarily exhilarated as he falls. But the moment he understands his true condition, he'll be terrified. If he has a backup parachute, his realization will serve him well.

Likewise, if this young man, overwhelmed with guilt, repented and embraced Christ's forgiveness, the crushing feelings of guilt that brought him to repentance would be God's grace to him—his parachute and only hope. Our God-given consciences are his gift to us, and when we don't repent of sin, our consciences are seared (see 1 Timothy 4:2).

We see a similar truth described in Proverbs 28:13: "People who conceal their sins will not prosper, but if they confess and turn from them, they will receive mercy" (NLT).

Confession Sets Us Free

Psalm 32, consisting of just eleven verses, is one of the saddest and happiest passages in all of Scripture. Here David sang about the misery of sin and the liberating happiness of confession and forgiveness.

David chose the sin of adultery with Bathsheba and subsequently murdered his loyal soldier Uriah to cover up his sin. He did what Satan convinced him would make him happy. What he found instead was abject misery.

Psalm 32 recounts David's heartfelt repentance, but before he describes his sin and misery, he is beside himself with joy. The psalm begins not with his sin but with something far greater still—God's forgiveness:

> Happy are those whose transgression is forgiven,
>   whose sin is covered.
> Happy are those to whom the LORD imputes
>   no iniquity,
>   and in whose spirit there is no deceit.
>
> PSALM 32:1-2, NRSV

Only after praising God did David talk about his sin, vividly describing his physical and mental condition before he confessed and repented:

> While I kept silence, my body wasted away
>   through my groaning all day long.
> For day and night your hand was heavy upon me;
>   my strength was dried up as by the heat of summer.
>
> PSALM 32:3-4, NRSV

But once David came to terms with his sin and turned to God, everything changed:

> Then I acknowledged my sin to you,
>   and I did not hide my iniquity;
> I said, "I will confess my transgressions to the LORD,"
>   and you forgave the guilt of my sin.
>
> PSALM 32:5, NRSV

David went on to describe his relationship with the God who delivered him from the unhappiness of guilt:

> You are a hiding place for me;
>   you preserve me from trouble;
>   you surround me with glad cries of deliverance.
>
> PSALM 32:7, NRSV

David finished his short song by contrasting the miseries of sin with the happiness of cleansing and forgiveness:

Many are the torments of the wicked,
>   but steadfast love surrounds those who trust
>   in the LORD.
Be glad in the LORD and rejoice, O righteous,
>   and shout for joy, all you upright in heart.

PSALM 32:10-11, NRSV

Spurgeon said, "It does not spoil your happiness . . . to confess your sin. The unhappiness is in not making the confession."[3]

Sin Never Pays

Grasping that sin is *never* in our best interests clarifies many otherwise difficult decisions.

Too often we imagine we must choose between helping people do what's right and helping them be happy. This is one of Satan's greatest lies.

For instance, a young woman I knew believed that abortion takes the life of an innocent child, but because she loved her friend, she was going to drive her to the clinic to get an abortion. She told me, "That's what you do when you love someone, even if you disagree."

I asked, "If your friend decided to kill her mother

and had a shotgun in hand, would you drive her to her mother's house?"

Eyes wide, she responded, angrily, "Of course not!"

But other than legality, what's the difference? Too often, in the name of love, we assist people in taking wrong actions which, *because* they're wrong, will rob them of happiness. We may congratulate ourselves for being "loving," but what good does our love do if our actions encourage and facilitate someone's self-destruction?

People imagine they are showing love to friends when they provide an alibi to their parents, facilitate an adulterous relationship, lie to a teacher or boss, create a distraction as they shoplift, or cover for them as they take drugs. But true friends don't enable and empower their friends to sin. They know that's not love, because it contributes not to their rescue and redemption but to their destruction.

God tells us the truth about what will make us happy. Our ultimate happiness hinges on whom we choose to believe—the devil who hates us or the God who loves us.

Forgiveness Is Powerful

Forgiving others affects our own forgiveness as well as our happiness.

Scripture instructs us, "Put on a heart of compassion, kindness, humility, gentleness and patience; bearing with one another, and forgiving each other, whoever has a complaint against anyone; just as the Lord forgave you, so also should you" (Colossians 3:12-13, NASB).

Christ tells the story of a servant who owes his king millions—a debt his ruler freely forgives. But when that servant refuses to forgive the debt of a fellow servant who owes him much less, the king says, "You wicked servant! I forgave you all that debt because you pleaded with me. And should not you have had mercy on your fellow servant, as I had mercy on you?" (Matthew 18:32-33).

The king delivers the man to the jailers until he can pay back his entire debt.

Jesus issues this sober warning: "So also my heavenly Father will do to every one of you, if you do not forgive your brother from your heart" (Matthew 18:35).

To say the least, God takes our failure to forgive seriously! There's no sin that Christ didn't die for, so there's no sin that we, in his strength, can't forgive. (That said, sometimes we must be realistic and exercise tough love.)

We may not forget all the facts of someone's offense, but we do not have to dwell on them. We must bury the sins of others, as God has buried ours.

The prophet Micah said to God, "You will again have compassion on us; you will tread our sins underfoot and hurl all our iniquities into the depths of the sea" (Micah 7:19, NIV).

Spurgeon said, "While we are young, perhaps we

are foolish enough to look elsewhere for happiness, but when we grow old and cares and sorrows increase, happy, indeed, are we if we have the happiness that comes from pardoned sin!"[4]

When we extend to others the forgiveness God has extended to us, not only do we receive happiness, we become conduits of happiness, spreading it wherever we go.

It Is Finished

Forgiveness and a restored relationship with God bring both relief from misery and an infusion of delight.

German Reformer Martin Luther (1483–1546) said, "Sin is pure unhappiness, forgiveness pure happiness."[5] It's hard to imagine a more concise and accurate statement about what will make us happy.

After enduring unthinkable agony on the cross, Jesus uttered these words: "It is finished" (John 19:30). These same words were commonly written across records of debt when paid in full. Moments later, Jesus—having done history's hardest task—bowed his head and died.

Whether we're completing a final class before graduating, finishing a huge construction job, or finalizing a big manuscript, saying, "It is finished," means the end of toil and the beginning of great celebration.

What can make us happier than contemplating the end of our separation from God because of what Jesus did? By his grace, others can forgive us—and we can look at those who have sinned against us and say, because of Christ's redemptive work, "It is finished. I hold no resentment, bitterness, or grudge. You are forgiven, and I am free!"

CHAPTER 11

IS HAPPINESS FOR NOW OR LATER . . . OR BOTH?

HAPPINESS SHOULD BE more than a pipe dream. The promise of eventual and eternal happiness is obviously good. But God doesn't intend for us to wait until we die to be happy!

Many passages call us to present-tense happiness—for instance, "How happy *is* [not *will be*] the one who does not walk in the advice of the wicked" (Psalm 1:1, CSB, emphasis added).

We are not told, "One day in Heaven you will rejoice in the Lord at last" but "Rejoice in the Lord always. I will say it again: Rejoice!" (Philippians 4:4, NIV). And if Paul could say that from prison, surely we can find many causes for rejoicing even on difficult days.

It's certainly true that the daily experience of happiness requires our sustained effort. When Nanci and I bought our house more than forty years ago, it didn't become ours in any meaningful sense until we took possession of it. Likewise, our happiness was bought and paid for by Christ. But until we take hold of it, it's not really ours.

Our Quest for Happiness Can't Be Passive

To find happiness, we must actively move toward it.

Consider Philippians 2:12-13: "Work out your own salvation with fear and trembling [our actions], for it is God who works in you [God's actions], both to will and to work for his good pleasure [God's actions]." We don't have to choose between God's sovereignty and human will; this passage teaches participation by both parties. (Naturally, any partnership between the infinite Creator God and finite, fallen human beings is decidedly unequal!)

We can't make ourselves happy in God any more than a seed can make itself grow. But we're not just seeds. We're greenhouse farmers who can make sure the seed is planted, watered, and fertilized.

Paul said to the church in Corinth, "I planted, Apollos watered, but God gave the growth" (1 Corinthians 3:6). While God makes the crop grow, the people who raise the largest and best produce, winning ribbons at the county fair, do their part too.

We Really Can Choose Happiness

It isn't easy, but it is always possible to choose what results in ultimate, lasting happiness.

Too many of us wait for sufficient motivation before making wise and joy-producing choices. But whether it's exercising, eating right, or volunteering to serve others, when we take those first steps toward embracing happiness, we overcome inertia and establish new habits. Once we see the happiness that results, we're much more motivated to keep up those new patterns.

Physical action, repeated over time, forms long-term muscle memory. Climbing, typing, hitting a tennis ball, and playing a musical instrument all utilize muscle memory. Happiness works in a similar way: the brain has its own muscle memory. We choose to follow Christ by taking a certain action, we find happiness in it, and then we do it again because of the payoff we receive.

For example, when we turn off the television and read a good, God-honoring book or a compelling story, we feel enriched. Recalling that engaging experience, we do the same thing again, and eventually it becomes a habit. We end up reading not just because we think we should but also because we want to better our lives.

Let's Choose Happiness

Both happiness and unhappiness are states of mind that self-perpetuate.

The more we choose delight and gratitude, the more delight and gratitude become our default. The more we choose anger and bitterness, the more anger and bitterness become our default.

Paul said, "Fix your thoughts on what is true. . . . Think about things that are excellent and worthy of praise" (Philippians 4:8, NLT). This process of retraining our thinking doesn't happen automatically. We have to cultivate the habit.

Most diets work when habitually followed, but no diet works when repeatedly violated. It's not the inherent virtue of a diet or exercise plan but the daily choices related to diet or exercise that determine results.

Some believers choose to obsess over everything that's wrong with the world. We're continually bombarded by "news" (often more sensational than informative) that dwells on life's suffering and tragedies. It's easy for the unceasing avalanche of bad news to bury the Good News.

I don't favor living in a cave, blissfully ignorant of the world's woes. But we honor our King when we focus our thoughts on true, eternal realities. We worship God by recognizing his presence, praying, and feeding our minds with his truths.

Political tribalism related to various news channels and talk shows encourages people to pick up their verbal torches and lay waste to anyone with an opposing viewpoint, throwing stones even at fellow believers who think differently than they do.

But what good does this do? Doesn't it just fuel our anger and rob us of perspective and peace? Instead, let's "encourage one another and build each other up" (1 Thessalonians 5:11, NIV).

If we would walk away from online disputes and pour the same amount of time and energy into helping those around us, God would be honored and we (and those we help) would be happier.

Worry Is a Happiness Thief

Worry is the product of high stakes and low control. Sometimes we imagine that if we care, we should worry—as if that will help. In fact, worry has absolutely no redemptive value and robs us of happiness. Jesus asked, "Who of you by worrying can add a single hour to your life?" (Luke 12:25, NIV).

Just after instructing us to rejoice in the Lord, Paul wrote in Philippians 4:6, "Do not be anxious about anything." Worry is a killjoy. It specializes in worst-case scenarios. In contrast, God tells his children there is much that should make us rejoice:

- He has already rescued us from the worst, which is eternal Hell.
- Even if something terrible happens, he uses it for our eternal good.
- Often bad things don't happen, and our worry proves groundless.
- Whether or not bad things happen, our worry helps nothing and hurts much.
- The cause of all our worries—sin and the Curse— is temporary and will soon be behind us. Forever.

The command to rejoice is not about pretense, unrealistic expectations, or positive thinking; it's grounded in an eternal reality.

Focus on the Positive

When I'm snorkeling for hours on end, taking underwater photos, I don't think about being cold, hungry, or tired. This is not because I'm in denial but because I'm so engrossed in the magnificent and praiseworthy creativity of my God, who made the ocean's wonders. Everything else pales in comparison.

When I was a child, I searched for unique and eyecatching rocks. There were lots of plain stones, as well as muddy ones, with worms and bugs all around and under them. But this didn't deter me, because I wasn't collecting worms or bugs; I was collecting beautiful stones. Even when they didn't appear beautiful, I saw their hidden beauty.

Just as I collected rocks, and as others collect coins and stamps, we can collect reasons to praise God. We can develop an eye for beauty in God, his world, and the people and man-made objects in it. That's not denying the Curse; it's cultivating and laying claim to the happiness of a God-centered worldview.

Even in a fallen world, God invites us to happiness in him. Why would we say no, when to say yes simply means making small decisions that produce significant results?

Does Happiness Come Naturally?

Happiness comes "naturally" only when we take steps to create the mental, spiritual, and physical environment that fosters it.

Happiness nearly always results when I take a bike ride or walk our dog or spend special time with Nanci. But sometimes that requires overcoming busyness, distractions, or inertia.

Sometimes we must set the stage for happiness—by inviting over a good friend, fixing a nice dinner, joining a small group, reading a good book, or going to church or Bible study even when we don't feel like it.

Our choices should be in concert with our prayers—praying to find happiness in God and then taking action to help us find happiness in him.

Some say, "I thought I would experience joy in the Christian life, but I never have." Is that because we spend hours a day on social media but "don't have time" to join a home Bible study? Do we manage to schedule business appointments, lunches, and tennis matches but not regular times with God?

Happiness comes naturally in the same sense that fruit comes naturally from a tree. If the tree gets sufficient sunshine and water, if the ground is rich in nutrients, if the tree doesn't contract diseases, then yes, it "naturally" produces fruit.

We must plant ourselves in the rich soil of God's Word, soak in the living water of God and his people, and bask in the radiant sunlight of his grace. We must take the steps to help and serve others, loving God and our neighbors. Only then, as we change our minds and actions, will newfound happiness come naturally.

There's No Magic Bullet for Happiness

The Christian life is supernatural but not enchanted. Scripture tells us we are to "be transformed by the renewing of [our] minds" (Romans 12:2, CEB). It calls on us to deliberately think about things that are good and praise-worthy (see Philippians 4:8).

God doesn't magically make us happy while we choose to think about what's bad and unworthy of praise. If we make work, sports, leisure, or sex into an idol, happiness will elude us. If we choose to seek happiness elsewhere, God won't force himself on us. And he certainly won't give us happiness in what distances us from him.

Why do we expect to be happy in God when we're not choosing to do what we can to learn, study, and discuss who God is, what he has done, what he's doing, and what he promises us?

Whose Voice Are You Listening To?

My conversion to Christ didn't just make me a better person; it made me a happier person. The closer I grow to Jesus, the deeper and greater my happiness. Not because I've seen less evil and suffering—indeed, I've seen far more than I did when I was less happy.

Over the years, I've learned that my intellectual life and spiritual life aren't on different tracks. They're inseparable—Jesus said we're to love the Lord our God with our hearts *and* our minds (see Matthew 22:37).

Our happiness is proportionate to our investment in God's Word. Had I not taken time to ponder God, his truth, and his ways, all the spiritual inclinations in the world wouldn't have left me with a settled happiness. "As your words came to me I drank them in, and they filled my heart with joy and happiness because I belong to you, O LORD, the God who rules over all" (Jeremiah 15:16, NET).

People are unhappy because they listen to the thousands of unhappy voices clamoring for their attention. Joy comes from listening to and believing words of joy from the Source of joy. Jesus said, "My sheep hear my voice, and I know them, and they follow me" (John 10:27). When we follow him, we're happy. When we don't, we're not.

Become a Happiness Expert

We all reflect on and talk about what's most important to us; the more happy-making that talk is, the happier we'll be. If we want to change what's important to us, we do so by investing more time in what matters.

Many Christian men would agree that they're experts in business, politics, hunting, fishing, basketball, fantasy football, or cars. What if they took even half the time they devote to political talk shows and hobbies and invested it in learning solid biblical doctrine through listening to the Bible and reading great Christian books?

There's nothing inherently wrong with an interest in sports and politics and the news. But being an expert in any of those doesn't prepare us to live wisely and compassionately or to make Christ-centered decisions or to lead our families through hard times or to die well. Time in God's Word does.

How many men have frequent God-centered conversations today—with each other, their wives, and their children? How much pleasure and happiness are we depriving ourselves of by talking about everything except what matters most?

Author and pastor Calvin Miller (1936–2012) lamented, "Our day is plagued by hordes of miserable Christians whose pitiful study habits give them few victories and much frustration. Serious students will develop dynamic minds and a confident use of the gifts God has given to them."[1]

Scripture promotes joy and liberation, not hostility and condemnation. On the one hand, the biblical law points out our unrighteousness, leading to our condemnation (see Romans 7:7). On the other hand, the life-giving aspect of that law—and the word *law* generally means "instruction"—caused David to happily celebrate it:

- I delight in your commands because I love them. (Psalm 119:47, NIV)
- I deeply love your Law! I think about it all day. (Psalm 119:97, CEV)

Spurgeon said, "There is nothing in the Law of God that will rob you of happiness—it only denies you that which would cost you sorrow!"[2]

God invites us to come to him and experience something wonderful, something that will take us deep into the knowledge of himself, which we will find saturates us with contentment and gladness: "Taste and see that the LORD is good. How happy is the man who takes refuge in Him!" (Psalm 34:8, HCSB).

Only by learning what Scripture says about God can we know what's true about him. That's how we can trust him more and experience the truth-based happiness that flows from him like rivers of living water.

CHAPTER 12

CAN WE BE HAPPY
DESPITE SUFFERING?

GOD NEVER GUARANTEES that the Christian life will be smooth or easy. In fact, he promises the opposite: "All who desire to live godly in Christ Jesus will suffer persecution" (2 Timothy 3:12, NKJV). We're not to be surprised when we face great difficulties (see 1 Peter 4:12).

All the psalms of lament, the book of Lamentations, and many other Scripture passages reveal the importance of realism and sorrow in the Christian life. No treatment of joy and happiness should deny or minimize such texts.

Indeed, a truly biblical worldview and an authentic doctrine of joy and happiness fully recognize and embrace the realities of suffering in this present age. The happiness described in Scripture is all the richer because it doesn't involve denial or pretense and can be experienced amid severe difficulty.

Christ-followers don't preach the flimsy kind of happiness that's built on wishful thinking. Instead, our basis for happiness remains true—and sometimes becomes clearer—in suffering.

Rejoicing Is Rooted in Our God, Not Our Circumstances

Rejoicing always in the Lord (see Philippians 4:4) may seem unrealistic at times. But we must remember that this rejoicing is centered not in a passing circumstance but in a constant reality—God himself, and his Son, Jesus, who died for us and rose again.

On the one hand, we might suppose that Scripture doesn't command us to rejoice in our nation's condition, our culture's trajectory, our spouse's attitude, our child's struggle, our church's conflicts, our job loss, or our poor health. On the other hand, we're told to "always [give] thanks to God the Father for everything, in the name of our Lord Jesus Christ" (Ephesians 5:20, NIV). Likewise, Scripture tells us to "give thanks in all circumstances; for this is God's will for you in Christ Jesus" (1 Thessalonians 5:18, NIV).

I don't think this means that we are to rejoice in evil, per se, since God hates evil (Zechariah 8:17; Proverbs 6:16-19) and commands us to hate it (Psalm 97:10;

Proverbs 8:13; Romans 12:9). I do think it means that we should believe Romans 8:28, which tells us God will work all things together for our good, including evil things that happen to us.

Believing this frees us to thank God in the middle of difficult and even evil circumstances, knowing that in his sovereign grace, he is accomplishing great, eternal purposes in us through these things.

We're told to rejoice *in the Lord* and to "consider it all joy" when we face hardship (James 1:2, NASB). Choosing to rejoice, by rehearsing reasons to be happy and grateful while suffering, affirms trust in God. We walk by faith, believing in what God has done, is doing, and will do to bring a good end to all that troubles us.

This response requires faith that God lovingly superintends our challenges. Viewing our sufferings as random or obsessing over someone else's bad choices that caused our sufferings robs us of happiness. A weak, small, or faulty view of God always poisons the well of our contentment.

Who is this God we are to trust? What is he really like? We won't trust him until we know him. Ours is a God with many attributes. If God were only sovereign, that wouldn't be enough. His power alone can't infuse us with happiness. His love is wonderful, but it, too, isn't enough.

Think about it. We could have an all-powerful God who doesn't love us. Or we could have a loving God who means well but doesn't have the power to make good things happen.

Instead, Scripture teaches that we have a God who loves us and is sovereign over the universe, including all evil. Our God promises us that he will cause all things, even our suffering, to work together for our ultimate good (see Romans 8:28).

The more we grow in our understanding of God's attributes, the happier we become.

We Have a Sovereign and Loving God

The deeper our knowledge of God's character, the deeper our reservoir of strength, perspective, and happiness in hard times.

We can't be happy, and remain happy, without believing in the sovereignty of a loving God. The beauty of the Christian worldview is that while we're encouraged to take initiative and control what's within our power, we also know that the enormous part of life we can't control is under God's governance.

I wrote the words in the previous paragraph before my wife, Nanci, was diagnosed with colon cancer in 2018. But now I find them even more important and true.

As much as we appreciate the physicians and the advances of medical science, our ultimate hope is not in them but in God. Trust in our sovereign and gracious and happy God, who alone is sufficient to bear the weight of our trust, allows Nanci and me to laugh and talk and pray together each night with an underlying foundation of happiness.

Even in the midst of seemingly endless trips to doctors and tests for white blood cell counts and round after round of chemotherapy, Nanci and I have both been delighting in God through delighting in his Word, and we have often discussed his character and faithfulness. He is the object of our faith and the source of our eternal perspective and present comfort.

Sure, there have been tears and discouragement at times. But these are eclipsed by our biblically grounded beliefs in an all-powerful Redeemer who cares for us so much that he went to the cross for us. (What more could we ask?)

Scripture tells us, "Our God is in the heavens; he does all that he pleases" (Psalm 115:3). It assures us, "The heart of man plans his way, but the LORD establishes his steps" (Proverbs 16:9). And since God is eternally wise and good and happy, and we're not, we're far better off with him, not us, in control.

We Can Find Peace in Suffering

All the circumstances we can't control rest in the Lord's hands. He is content and peaceful and happy, and our contentment, peace, and happiness derive from his.

As we deal with her cancer, Nanci and I have spent

time meditating on the attributes of God, rereading and listening to audiobooks such as *The Knowledge of the Holy* by A. W. Tozer and *Knowing God* by J. I. Packer and *Trusting God* by Jerry Bridges. Our hearts are lifted in praise as we contemplate his holiness, grace, justice, mercy, and every facet of his being revealed to us in Scripture.

One of the first passages I memorized forty-five years ago as a young Christian is more real and more encouraging to me in this trial than it has ever been:

> Do not be anxious about anything, but in everything by prayer and supplication with thanksgiving let your requests be made known to God. And the peace of God, which surpasses all understanding, will guard your hearts and your minds in Christ Jesus.
>
> PHILIPPIANS 4:6-7

That amazing peace seems to defy the challenges and uncertainties of our present circumstances.

In our fallen world, troubles and difficulties are constants. Happy people look beyond their circumstances to someone so big that by his grace, even great difficulties become manageable—and provide opportunities for a deeper kind of happiness.

Gratitude Is Central

Choosing to be thankful always raises the level of our happiness.

In every circumstance, no matter how difficult, we can give thanks to God and experience his joy. Ephesians 5:18-20 says, "Be filled with the Spirit, addressing one another in psalms and hymns and spiritual songs, singing and making melody to the Lord with your heart, giving thanks always and for everything to God the Father in the name of our Lord Jesus Christ." Being Spirit controlled is inseparable from giving thanks in everything.

Since unhappiness comes as we focus on life's downsides, and thankfulness affirms its upsides, thankfulness is the greatest antidote to unhappiness.

When Nanci and I recently had to cancel a trip we were really looking forward to, we began to contemplate all the good things that we could do with the time we now had. Then we started doing those good things and got excited about them. Instead of clinging to unhappiness for something we lost, we found happiness in something we gained.

Whether we find ourselves having reason to celebrate or to mourn, there's never a time not to express our gratitude to God. Psalm 140:13 declares, "Surely the righteous shall give thanks to your name." Giving thanks is what God's people do.

Ann Voskamp writes,

As long as thanks is possible, then joy is always possible. *Joy is always possible. Whenever*, meaning—now; *wherever*, meaning—here. The holy grail of joy is not in some exotic location or some emotional mountain peak experience. The joy wonder could be here! Here, in the messy, piercing ache of now, joy might be— unbelievably—possible![1]

While it may seem hard to "make ourselves happy," it's not hard to choose to give thanks, which in turn always kindles happiness. No matter how difficult our circumstances, the happiness thanksgiving generates is always within our reach.

Let's Contemplate Our Spiritual Circumstances

When we talk about our circumstances, we usually mean the temporal, outward conditions of our lives. These may include a lost job, estranged relationships, illness, fatigue, or depression.

But if we are in Christ, we should look to and affirm our "spiritual circumstances," which are eternal and very real. We are created by God, loved by him, redeemed by Christ, indwelt with and empowered by his Spirit, assured of an eternally happy and abundant life. No one can snatch us out of God's hands. We are more than conquerors through Christ, he is working all things together for our good, and nothing will ever separate us from his love!

Ponder *those* circumstances, every day and every hour, and they will overshadow your temporal circumstances.

Yes, our present circumstances *do* matter. But in the scope of eternity, instead of determining our happiness, they offer opportunities for our growth and ultimate good. When they threaten to overwhelm us, difficult circumstances can remind us to look to God, our Rock and Redeemer, who is our happiness.

Happiness Is Not Indifference

If you're going through great suffering right now, the message "God is always happy" may disturb you. You might react the way you would if you told a friend, "My daughter was just diagnosed with leukemia," and your friend replied, "I'm always happy, so I won't let that bother me."

God's happiness, though uninterrupted, should never be misconstrued as indifference. Although he is happy and wants us to be happy, he is still moved by our sorrows.

We're told of God, in relationship with his people, "In all their affliction he was afflicted. . . . In his love and in his pity he redeemed them; he lifted them up and carried them all the days of old" (Isaiah 63:9). What a moving portrayal of the tenderness of his affection for us and devotion to us!

God himself models his inspired command to rejoice always. He sympathizes with all his suffering children, but he rejoices in purchasing our redemption and making us more like Jesus. He joyfully prepares a place for us, and he has eternally happy plans. He has the power to accomplish everything, as well as the sure knowledge that it will happen.

While I'm grateful that God cares deeply for me, I'm also glad that when I'm miserable, it doesn't mean God is. Any good father will be moved by his daughter's pain if her fiancé calls off their wedding. But even a human father may be able to put it in perspective and realize that this is ultimately best.

God our Father, infinitely wise, can feel our pain while retaining his own happiness. He has an infinitely larger picture than any human father of the eventual, eternal good that he will certainly accomplish. Nothing is outside his control.

Suffering Has Purpose

There is nothing that so undermines happiness as the misperception that the world is hopeless and suffering is pointless. But for God's children, there is never pointless suffering.

Of course, much pain may appear pointless since we are finite and fallen, incapable of understanding the purposes of God in his infinite wisdom. Job must have understood this as he cried out in his agony, "Though he slay me, yet will I trust in him" (Job 13:15, KJV).

What does our suffering do for us, then, whether it is suffering for Christ or the ordinary suffering of life in a sin-stained world? It helps us see the implausibility of finding true happiness outside of God. When what we once leaned on for happiness—even if it's something well meaning, such as acceptance from family and friends—crumbles into dust, we can finally see that God stands firm as the one solid foundation on which to build our lives and happiness.

Our Suffering Will End

Even if the worst suffering of our lives still lies ahead of us, our loving God assures us it will be for only a short time. But he promises far more—a future payoff for our present sufferings:

- Our present sufferings are not worth comparing with the glory that will be revealed in us. (Romans 8:18, NIV)
- Our light and momentary troubles are achieving for us an eternal glory that far outweighs them all. (2 Corinthians 4:17, NIV)

In light of that eternal glory being achieved for us by our momentary troubles, Paul offers the following words of eternal perspective: "We fix our eyes not on what is seen, but on what is unseen, since what is seen is temporary, but what is unseen is eternal" (2 Corinthians 4:18, NIV). This verse has always cleared my head, and that's why I named our organization Eternal Perspective Ministries.

How wonderful to be promised not only that our present sufferings will end but also that even now they have a hidden purpose that will forever outlast this life! The more we fix our eyes on what's presently unseen, the more we can experience reassurance and comfort and the increase in happiness they inevitably bring.

We desperately need the constant awareness that we aren't living primarily for the here and now. That's why Scottish evangelist Duncan Matheson (1824–1869) prayed, "Lord, stamp eternity upon my eyeballs."[2]

A normal day as resurrected people on the New Earth will be far better than the best day we've ever experienced here. And we will one day see our worst day on Earth under the Curse as not having been wasted but as making a positive and eternal difference.

CHAPTER 13

WILL WE REALLY
LIVE HAPPILY EVER AFTER?

NEARLY EVERY MYTH, legend, and utopian prophecy expresses the hope that Earth and its inhabitants will be restored to the happiness we instinctively know was somehow tragically lost.

"They all lived happily ever after" is more than a fairy-tale ending. It's the deep-seated dream of the human race.

In AD 60, Seneca (c. 4 BC–AD 65), the Roman Stoic philosopher and statesman who advised Nero, wrote, "No happiness lasts for long."[1] At the same time in history, the apostle Paul and others were spreading the good news that happiness in God lasts not just a long time but forever.

In Rome, about five years later, both by Nero's decree, first Seneca and then Paul were executed. Three years later, when the political tide turned against him, Nero killed himself. Since as far as we know the evil emperor didn't repent and turn to Christ, whatever meager happiness he knew ended forever at his death.

So Seneca was right when he said happiness is short lived . . . *unless* the Bible is true and death is not the end of us or the world; a happy God has purchased his people's redemption; and a happy, resurrected life in a resurrected world awaits those who trust Jesus for their eternal well-being. Those who believe this—I'm among them, and I hope you are too—know the happiness that will last forever.

For people with no faith in Jesus, these are their best days ever, winding down to a fixed end. But for genuine Christ-followers, these are decidedly *not* the best days of our lives. Jesus has promised us eternal, abundant life, with the best by far yet to come.

We Will Experience Eternal Joy

A. W. Tozer said, "When the followers of Jesus Christ lose their interest in heaven they will no longer be happy Christians, and when they are no longer happy Christians they cannot be a powerful force in a sad and sinful world. It may be said with certainty that Christians who have lost their enthusiasm about the Savior's promises of heaven-to-come have also stopped being effective in Christian life and witness in this world."[2]

A culturally engaged young man, a bestselling Christian author with a large following, interviewed me concerning my book *Heaven*. Before the interview, he told me apologetically, "Truth is, I didn't read your book."

I had read his books, so I smiled and said, "Let me guess why. You think Heaven will be boring, and it's the beauties and wonders of this life—the natural world and human culture and the arts—that you're really interested in."

Obviously surprised, he said, "Yes!"

"That's exactly why you should read the book," I said. "It's about the New Earth the Bible reveals, a place with resurrected people on a resurrected planet; with resurrected nature, nations, and cultures; with animals, art, music, literature, drama, galaxies, and planets—all existing for the glory of God and the good of his people."

He smiled broadly, and his eyes brightened a moment before fading, as if to say, "If only that were true."

Well, it *is* true. The gospel—the Good News—is way better than we believe it to be. If we pay attention when we read the Bible, we'll see it:

Be happy and rejoice forevermore over what I am
about to create! For look, I am ready to create
Jerusalem to be a source of joy, and her people to

be a source of happiness. Jerusalem will bring me
joy, and my people will bring me happiness. The
sound of weeping or cries of sorrow will never be
heard in her again.

ISAIAH 65:18-19, NET

Death Is Not the End

For Christians, death is not the end of our adventure.
Rather, death is the doorway from a world where dreams
and adventures shrink, into a far better world where they
forever expand.

We normally think of going up to Heaven to live with
God in his place. Indeed, that happens when we die and
go to the present Heaven. But God ultimately promises
to come live with us in our place, on the New Earth. The
final state will not be "us with God" but "God with us"
(see Revelation 21:3).

The best part of our resurrected lives on the New
Earth will be seeing God. "No longer will there be any
curse. The throne of God and of the Lamb will be in the
city, and his servants will serve him. They will see his face"
(Revelation 22:3-4, NIV).

Based on this and other passages, ancient theologians
often spoke of the "beatific vision," from three Latin
words that together mean "a happy-making sight."

Because God is the fountainhead of all happiness, and

because he's forever happy in his triune oneness, to gaze on him will be to enter into happiness.

We Won't Become Ghosts

One of the greatest gifts we can give our children and grandchildren is to teach them the doctrines of the Resurrection and the New Earth. God made us to be physical beings in a physical world, living meaningful lives—eating, drinking, playing, working, loving, worshiping, and laughing to God's glory. That's the promise of the Resurrection—eternal delight and joy in the presence of the God who redeemed us.

Imagine sitting around campfires on the New Earth, wide eyed at the adventures being recounted. Yes, I'm talking about real stories around real campfires. After all, friendship, camaraderie, laughter, stories, and campfires are all good gifts from God for physical people living in a physical world . . . and the Bible tells us that's what we'll be and where we'll be!

On the New Earth, we may experience adventures that make our current rock climbing, surfing, skydiving, and upside-down roller-coaster rides seem tame. Why do I say this? It's an argument from design. We take pleasure in exhilarating experiences not because of sin but because God wired us this way. We weren't made to sit all day in dark rooms watching actors pretend to live.

Perhaps an alarm is going off in your head: *But that's unspiritual. We should only want to be with Jesus.* Well, seeing Jesus should certainly be at the top of the list. But that doesn't mean the other things God promises shouldn't be on the list—things he tells us are ahead, things that fully honor him and flow out of his grace and kindness to us.

We'll Inhabit Earth as It Was Meant to Be

Imagine the delight of Jesus' disciples when he said to them, "At the renewal of all things, when the Son of Man sits on his glorious throne, you who have followed me will also sit on twelve thrones, judging the twelve tribes of Israel" (Matthew 19:28, NIV).

Christ did not speak of the destruction or abandonment of all things but their *renewal*. That word affirms continuity between the past, present, and future Earth. The old world is the new world that will be radically refurbished to an even greater version of its original self.

God designed humans to live on Earth to his glory. Christ's incarnation, life, death, and resurrection secured a New Earth, where life will be the way God always intended.

Similarly, Peter preached that Christ must remain in Heaven "until the time comes for God to restore everything, as he promised long ago through his holy prophets" (Acts 3:21, NIV). This cosmic restoration is not God bringing disembodied people to fellowship with him in a spirit realm. Rather, it's God returning humankind to what he designed us to be. The entire physical universe will not just go back to its pre-Fall glory but will go forward to something even more magnificent.

Spurgeon explained the gospel this way:

> Now that Jesus Christ has come to restore the ruins of the Fall, He has come to bring back to us the old joy—only it shall be even sweeter and deeper than it could have been if we had never lost it! A Christian has never fully realized what Christ came to make him until he has grasped the joy of the Lord. Christ wishes His people to be happy.[3]

Sadly, most of us don't live as if we believe in God's promise of a New Earth.

Hanging on, white knuckled, to this life proves our disbelief in an afterlife that is physical (with real health), material (with real wealth), social (with real culture and relationships), and personal (with real happiness, fulfillment, and continuity of identity).

Despite Scripture's claim to the contrary, even Christians end up thinking, *If I can't live my dreams now, I never will.*

How easily we buy into Satan's lie: "You only go around once . . ." But if we know Jesus, we actually go around twice—and the second time lasts forever. It's called eternal life, and we will live it in resurrected bodies in a redeemed universe, on a New Earth, with King Jesus!

There's No Need for Bucket Lists

Life after death will afford us unlimited opportunities to enjoy with physical bodies and renewed minds a renewed physical universe. Tomorrow will never disappoint us, because, as C. S. Lewis said of the world to come, "every chapter is better than the one before."[4]

My friend Calvin Miller wrote about the world that awaits us:

> *I once scorned ev'ry fearful thought of death,*
> *When it was but the end of pulse and breath,*
> *But now my eyes have seen that past the pain*
> *There is a world that's waiting to be claimed.*
> *Earthmaker, Holy, let me now depart,*
> *For living's such a temporary art.*
> *And dying is but getting dressed for God,*
> *Our graves are merely doorways cut in sod.*[5]

I've heard it said, "We can't begin to imagine Heaven and what life will be like there." Certainly, our imaginations can't presently do it justice, but we can, in fact, imagine it, based on what Scripture tells us.

If we fail to imagine Heaven, it won't appeal to us and we won't anticipate it as we should. If we eagerly await vacations and what we're going to see and do, how much more should we anticipate our eternal life with King Jesus!

Puritan pastor Richard Baxter (1615–1691) said,

> Can you think that anything is fitter for the chiefest of your thoughts and cares, than the God and kingdom, which you hope for ever to enjoy? Or is there anything that can be more suitable, or should be more delightful to your thoughts, than to employ them about your highest hopes, upon your endless happiness and joy?[6]

Not only does putting our hope in Jesus and clinging to his blood-bought promises make the tunnel endurable, it gives us something to look forward to when we emerge. Not just into a better world, but into a new and perfect world. A world alive, fresh, beautiful, and devoid of pain, suffering, and war; a world without disease, accident, and tragedy; a world without dictators and madmen. A world ruled by King Jesus—the only one worthy to rule.

In reflecting on his life's work, which included *Les Misérables*, writer Victor Hugo spoke with excitement of anticipating the work he would do for God in the eternal state:

> I feel within me that future life. I am like a forest that has been razed; the new shoots are stronger and brighter. I shall most certainly rise toward the heavens. . . . The nearer my approach to the end, the plainer is the sound of immortal symphonies of worlds which invite me. For half a century I have been translating my thoughts into prose and verse: history, philosophy, drama, romance, tradition, satire, ode, and song; all of these I have tried. But I feel I haven't given utterance to the thousandth part of what lies within me. When I go to the grave I can say, as others have said, "My day's work is done." But I cannot say, "My life is done." My work will recommence the next morning. The tomb is not a blind alley; it is a thoroughfare. It closes upon the twilight, but opens upon the dawn.[7]

This Is Not Our Last Chance for Happiness

This life is neither our only opportunity nor our best one for happiness, adventure, and fun.

I've read books on happiness stressing that we must be

happy right here and now, living in the moment, because this is our one and only chance. How sad!

Thankfully, God says otherwise. His people will have an eternity of present *and* future happiness. Anticipation of an upcoming vacation or adventure brings us delight even in the midst of busyness and fatigue. On a larger scale, God's assurance of our never-ending happiness in his presence, on the New Earth, should front-load Heaven's joy into our lives today.

Ponder this reality until it floods your heart with gladness: Jesus will be the center of everything. Happiness will be the lifeblood of our resurrected lives.

And just when we think, *It doesn't get any better than this*, it will!

CHAPTER 14

HOW CAN HAPPINESS TRANSFORM US, OUR FAMILIES, AND OUR CHURCHES?

AMONG CHRISTIANS, there are two extremes when it comes to happiness.

Some change the channel from coverage of a hurricane, refuse to think about sex trafficking and abortion, and ignore the sufferings of this world while grabbing on to superficial living. They look the other way when their marriages are in trouble or when their children choose wrong friends, yet they keep clinging to the expectation that trusting Jesus means they are entitled to easy lives without suffering.

Other Christians are perpetually somber and angry, never laughing or poking fun at themselves, rarely celebrating, and quick to frown when they see someone having fun. Shoulders sagging, they believe that *happiness* is entirely unrealistic or is just another word for *ungodliness*.

The Bible presents a far more balanced perspective. Paul said he was "sorrowful, yet always rejoicing" (2 Corinthians 6:10). Sorrow and joy are *not* mutually exclusive, though for God's children, sorrow is temporary and joy will be eternal. (Note that the "always" in this verse applies to rejoicing, not being sorrowful.)

Why Do Christians Have a Reputation for Unhappiness?

Many people perceive Christianity as stodgy, sour-faced moralism, not the happiness of abundant life. Reformer John Calvin said, "While all men seek after happiness, scarcely one in a hundred looks for it from God."[1]

Why is that? Our first problem is that we're sinners, so our hearts are bent toward rebellion. But our second problem is that, based on what we've heard our whole lives, whether outside or inside the church, we'd never guess we can find happiness in God.

Author G. K. Chesterton (1874–1936) has been widely credited with saying, "Jesus promised His disciples three things—that they would be completely fearless, absurdly happy, and in constant trouble." It might be argued that most Western Christians aren't any of these three—least of all "absurdly happy."

I've taught college courses on biblical ethics, and I make no apologies for believing in Christian morality. But some Christians, in the name of moral obligation, go around with frowns on their faces, dutifully living a paint-by-numbers religious existence. They seem to wear their displeasure as a badge of honor.

Ironically, the church has made unbelievers fear that becoming Christians will make them unhappy. They've known—as many of us churchgoers have also known—professing Christians who go out of their way to promote misery, not gladness.

I've seen Bible-believing, Christ-centered people post comments on blogs or social media only to receive a string of outraged responses from people who wield Scripture like a pickax, swiftly condemning the slightest hint of a viewpoint they consider suspicious. When I was an unbeliever, such responses certainly wouldn't have drawn me to the Christian faith.

I wonder why those engaging in such behavior don't immediately recognize how their actions utterly contradict the faith they profess and the Bible they believe and the Lord they seem determined to speak for.

Why are perpetual disdain, suspicion, unkindness, snarkiness, and hostility seen by some as taking the spiritual high ground? Perhaps these joy snipers are living out the lie that Christians shouldn't be happy!

Grim-faced pharisaical "Christians" make Satan's propaganda campaign far easier by misrepresenting God, undermining the Good News, and promoting a negative view of happiness.

Who would ever be drawn to the worldview of decidedly unhappy people? Curmudgeonly Christianity pulls no one to Jesus and pushes many away.

Shouldn't Christianity Bring Joy to the World?

In most unbelievers' perceptions, Christianity hasn't brought much joy to the world. As a religion, it's primarily known for its rules, self-righteousness, and intolerance—none of which convey gladness and merriment.

Of course, this is neither the whole story nor even the main story. Throughout history, the Christian worldview has accounted for many happiness-generating developments such as hospitals and schools, science and industry, music, drama, and the arts.

On a more personal level, nearly every community includes people whose quiet confidence in Christ, extraordinary love, kindness, helpfulness, and cheer make their world a better place. They gladly give of their time and money to those in need. Their impact is real and profound, and their happiness contagious.

Unfortunately, because such people are rarely in the public eye, they appear as the exception rather than the rule. The public perception of Christianity is that it is dominated by harsh and proud negativity.

Thomas Aquinas (1225–1274), the most influential theologian of the Middle Ages, wrote, "Man is unable not to wish to be happy."[2] This means that all attempts by Christians to disregard or demean happiness are misguided and unfruitful. By creating distance between the gospel and happiness, we send the unbiblical (and historically ungrounded) message that the Christian faith is dull and dreary.

Let's speak against sin but hold up Christ as the happiness everyone longs for. If we don't, we will assure our own unhappiness and feed the world's perception that Christianity subtracts happiness instead of multiplying it.

Let's Preach the Good News of Happiness

Why shouldn't churches teach and live out the biblical doctrine of God's happiness and ours?

Why shouldn't churches encourage their members to memorize and meditate on the countless biblical passages about happiness in God?

Why shouldn't pastors preach on and even have annual series of messages on passages such as "Let all those who seek You rejoice and be glad in You; let such as love Your salvation say continually, 'The LORD be magnified!'" (Psalm 40:16, NKJV)?

There are easily a hundred other happiness passages, a number of them mentioned in this book, that lend themselves to being taught and preached. For those like me who don't like superficial or trendy messages but ones that dig deep into God's Word, consider as one example what could be done in preaching Zephaniah 3.

In Zephaniah 3:14, God calls on his people to be glad using four different Hebrew words that each convey happiness: "Sing aloud [with joy, or *rinnah*[3]], O daughter of Zion; shout [for joy, or *ruah*[4]], O Israel! Rejoice [*samach*] and exult [*alaz*] with all your heart."

The gladness described in this verse is over the top—surely a God who isn't happy would never call his people to such happiness. But we're not left to speculate, because just three verses later, in Zephaniah 3:17, we see an even more remarkable statement, also containing four Hebrew words for happiness. (This could be a great follow-up sermon.)

In this verse, all four terms are used not of God's people but of God himself: "The LORD your God is in your midst, a mighty one who will save; he will rejoice [*sus*] over you with gladness [*simchah*]; he will quiet you by his love; he will exult [*gyl*] over you with loud singing [*rinnah*]."

There's more of God's happiness, tenderness, and love in this single verse than we can wrap our minds around.

In fact, this understanding about God's delight in us is the rock-solid foundation for the fourfold happiness he calls on his people to experience three verses earlier.

Church people are accustomed to thinking of God as angry or saddened by us. But here we're told, four times over, of God's happiness over us! In regard to this passage, A. W. Tozer said words we should echo: "God is happy if nobody else is."[5] But the best reason for us to be happy is because *he* is.

The truth about God's happiness needs to first be privately believed, but then it needs to be publicly declared and celebrated! And when it's made public long enough, it will become the settled belief of countless Christians.

Our Happiness Should Overflow

Charles Spurgeon told his church, "There is so much misery in this world that none of us ought to add to it. . . . Let us, on the contrary, seek to increase happiness and joy wherever we can!"[6] How might happy Christians be a positive force for evangelism and cultural change?

Imagine churches known as communities of Jesus-centered happiness, overflowing with the sheer gladness of embracing and living out the good news of great joy.

Imagine children bringing friends to church and hearing them comment, "Those people are so happy!" Wouldn't this infuse the gospel with a meaning that most of the world has never heard and even many of God's people have never known?

I'm not talking about the superficial happiness of over-eager church greeters with toothy smiles cornering people as a strategy for church growth. I mean the genuine happiness that naturally flows from God and the gospel. I'm talking about teaching a Bible that's full of celebrations and centered on a Messiah whose first miracle was to save a party by turning water into wine.

A. W. Tozer wrote, "The people of God ought to be the happiest people in all the wide world! People should be coming to us constantly and asking the source of our joy and delight."[7]

Are unbelievers coming to us constantly and asking us that question? If not, why not?

Happiness Is Contagious

Envision how contagious the doctrine of God's happiness would be if lived out. Imagine if we, though tired and stressed, wanted to gather with the church not out of sheer duty but because it brings more happiness than anything else we can think to do—way more, for instance, than staying home and watching television or spending time online.

What if our children saw in our families and churches a breadth of Christ-centered, optimistic happiness and were taught that this happiness originates in God, not the world? How might it fulfill these words: "That the generation to come might know, even the children yet to be born, that they may arise and tell them to their children, that they should put their confidence in God" (Psalm 78:6-7, NASB)?

What if people heard their pastors say what Spurgeon said to his church in London 150 years ago: "Those who are 'beloved of the Lord' must be the most happy and joyful people to be found anywhere upon the face of the earth"[8]?

What if when our families left church and went to school, work, restaurants, and musical or dramatic performances, they didn't feel they were walking away from God but toward the same happy God they've been worshiping?

What if, when suffering came, we faced it with an underlying faith that demonstrates genuine gladness in God and thanksgiving to God? What if our tears were often interspersed with laughter? What if our model was Jesus, who both wept over the death of his friend Lazarus (see John 11:35) and "rejoiced in the Holy Spirit" (Luke 10:21)?

What if, instead of looking away from or being paralyzed by the needs of this world, we—with humility and gladness—reached out to intervene for the hungry, the sick, the unborn, the persecuted, and those facing racial or gender discrimination?

Wouldn't our children be less likely to leave the Christian faith, push away church as a bad memory, and pursue the world's inferior happiness substitutes that will ultimately destroy them? Suppose evangelical churches invited our neighbors to celebrate with us on October 4, the Feast of Saint Francis, recognizing God as the Creator of animals, including their beloved pets and ours? Together we could celebrate the God who makes animals and loves and delights in them—and made us to do the same.

Imagine Jesus-followers leading the way in celebrating March 20 as the International Day of Happiness, a day officially recognized by all 192 countries of the United Nations. What an opportunity to tell each other and the world about why we celebrate happiness—because God is happy, happiness is his gift to us, and Christ came to bring happiness to people of every tribe, nation, and language!

Let's Start a Happiness Movement

Wouldn't it be refreshing for Christians to take the lead in speaking of and directing people to the happy God?

Wouldn't it be great if children growing up in Christian homes looked forward to some new God-centered holidays—ones they could invite their unbelieving friends to join?

Wouldn't it be fitting if the church was known for celebrating more than the world, rather than less? Worship, camaraderie, and unity would be hallmarks of such celebrations. But one of the greatest payoffs would be reestablishing followers of Jesus as people of profound happiness who are quick to celebrate the greatness, goodness, love, grace, and happiness of our God.

What if we really believed that the gospel offers not just what everyone needs but what, in the depths of our hearts, we truly want?

Think of the refreshment that weary, burdened, guilt-ridden people would enjoy if the church put on regular celebrations of biblical proportions, with great food and drink and music and laughter and fun, just to say, "We love you, Lord Jesus, and we're here to celebrate together who you are and all you've done for us!"

Spread the Good News

Let's look for every opportunity to share the Good News of God's happiness!

Once we've experienced the biblically based and delightful truth that God wants us to be happy, we have the privilege and the joyful obligation to share that revelation with others.

If God's happiness truly spilled into and out of his people, make no mistake: our children and grandchildren and communities would know it. Happiness in Christ is irrepressible.

Sure, if we believe and teach God's Word, we'll suffer and be criticized. But if God's happiness permeated us, wouldn't far more of the happiness-seeking world be attracted to Jesus?

May it be said of us that because of the happy God we know, the Jesus we love, the gospel we embrace, and the treasure we gladly share, we are truly the happiest people in the world.

And may we see our present happiness as a down payment on the eternal happiness that awaits us, bought and paid for by the blood of Christ, who is eager to welcome us into his happiness—a happiness that had no beginning and will have no end.

> The people the LORD has freed will return and
> enter Jerusalem with joy. Their happiness will
> last forever. They will have joy and gladness,
> and all sadness and sorrow will be gone far away.
>
> ISAIAH 51:11, NCV

Notes

CHAPTER 1: DOES GOD CARE ABOUT OUR HAPPINESS?

1. Thomas A. Hand, *St. Augustine on Prayer* (South Bend, IN: Newman Press, 1963), 1.
2. Blaise Pascal, *Pensées*, number 425.
3. Thomas Boston, *The Whole Works of the Late Reverend and Learned Mr. Thomas Boston*, vol. 1.
4. George Whitefield, "Worldly Business No Plea for the Neglect of Religion," *Selected Sermons of George Whitefield*.
5. Whitefield, "The Folly and Danger of Parting with Christ for the Pleasures and Profits of Life," *Selected Sermons of George Whitefield*.
6. Charles H. Spurgeon, "God Rejoicing in the New Creation" (Sermon #2211).
7. Anugrah Kumar, "LifeChurch.tv Pastor Craig Groeschel Says God Doesn't Want You Happy," *Christian Post*, February 9, 2015, http://www.christianpost.com/news/lifechurch-tv-pastor-craig-groeschel-says-god-doesnt-want-you-happy-133795/.
8. David P. Gushee and Robert H. Long, *A Bolder Pulpit: Reclaiming the Moral Dimension of Preaching* (Valley Forge, PA: Judson Press, 1998), 194.

CHAPTER 2: IS GOD HAPPY?

1. J. C. Ryle, *Happiness: The Secret of Happiness as Found in the Bible* (Cedar Lake, MI: Waymark Books, 2011), 7.

2. Michael Reeves, *Delighting in the Trinity* (Downers Grove, IL: InterVarsity Press, 2012), 16.

3. Steve DeWitt, *Eyes Wide Open: Enjoying God in Everything* (Grand Rapids, MI: Credo House, 2012), 46–47.

4. Charles H. Spurgeon, "Adorning the Gospel" (Sermon #2416).

CHAPTER 3: WHO WAS THE HAPPIEST PERSON IN HUMAN HISTORY?

1. John Gill, "Commentary on Proverbs," *John Gill's Exposition of the Bible*.

2. Charles Bridges, *An Exposition of the Book of Proverbs* (New York: Robert Carter & Brothers, 1850), 64.

3. Derek Kidner, *The Proverbs: An Introduction and Commentary*, The Tyndale Old Testament Commentaries (Downers Grove, IL: InterVarsity Press, 1984), 79.

4. Tremper Longman III, *How to Read Proverbs* (Downers Grove, IL: InterVarsity Press, 2002), 107.

5. Dylan Demarsico, "In the Beginning Was Laughter," *Christianity Today*, September 18, 2014.

6. John Piper, *Seeing and Savoring Jesus Christ* (Wheaton, IL: Crossway, 2004), 36.

7. Samuel Lamerson, "Jesus Never Laughed?" *Bible Study Magazine* (blog), November 19, 2014, http://www.biblestudymagazine.com/bible-study-magazine-blog/2014/11/19/jesus-never-laughed.

8. Leland Ryken, James C. Wilhoit, and Tremper Longman III, eds., "Humor—Jesus as Humorist," *Dictionary of Biblical Imagery* (Downers Grove, IL: InterVarsity Press, 1998), 410.

9. Ibid.

10. See footnote on Matthew 25:15, *ESV Study Bible* (Wheaton, IL: Crossway, 2008).

11. See note on Matthew 18:24, *The NET Bible* (Biblical Studies Press, 2006).

12. Elton Trueblood, *The Humor of Christ* (New York: Harper & Row, 1964), 9.

CHAPTER 4: WHAT ARE SOME CHRISTIAN MYTHS ABOUT HAPPINESS?

1. Edward Leigh, *A Treatise of Divinity: Consisting of Three Bookes*, Booke 2.

2. Thomas Brooks, "An Ark for All God's Noahs," *The Complete Works of Thomas Brooks*, vol. 2.

3. John Wesley, "Spiritual Worship" (Sermon #82).

4. Ibid.

5. Spiros Zodhiates, *The Pursuit of Happiness: An Exegetical Commentary on the Beatitudes*, rev. ed. (Chattanooga, TN: AMG, 1976).

6. D. A. Carson, *Exegetical Fallacies* (Grand Rapids, MI: Baker Academic, 1996), 32.

7. Charles H. Spurgeon, "The Christian's Badge," *Able to the Uttermost: Twenty Gospel Sermons*.

8. Oswald Chambers, *Biblical Ethics* (Great Britain: Oswald Chambers Publications, 1947), 14.

9. Chambers, *God's Workmanship and He Shall Glorify Me* (Grand Rapids, MI: Discovery House, 1997), 346.

10. Chambers, *My Utmost for His Highest* (Grand Rapids, MI: Discovery House, 2006), 31.

11. "In Your Opinion, What's the Difference between Joy and Happiness?" *Yahoo! Answers*, https://answers.yahoo.com/question/index?qid=20070926074249AAEJsKt.

12. For a much more thorough study of this topic, see *Happiness*, by Randy Alcorn (Carol Stream, IL: Tyndale House, 2015).

CHAPTER 5: ARE JOY AND HAPPINESS AT ODDS WITH EACH OTHER?

1. Dorcas Willis, *The Journey Called Ministry* (Bloomington, IN: AuthorHouse, 2013), 41.

2. Celeste P. Walker, *Joy: The Secret of Being Content* (Hagerstown, MD: Review and Herald, 2005), 65.

3. S. D. Gordon, quoted in Billy Graham, *Peace with God: The Secret of Happiness* (Nashville: Thomas Nelson, 2000), 202.

4. Kristin Jack, "Jesus Doesn't Want You to Be Happy," Urbana Student Missions Conferences blog, October 11, 2005, http://urbana.org/go-and-do/missional-life/jesus-doesnt-want-you-be-happy.

5. John Piper, "Let Your Passion Be Single," *Desiring God*, November 12, 1999, http://www.desiringgod.org/conference-messages/let-your-passion-be-single.

6. *Merriam-Webster Unabridged Dictionary* (Britannica Digital Learning, 2014), s.v. "joy," http://www.merriam-webster.com/dictionary/joy.

7. Isaac Watts, *The Psalms and Hymns of Isaac Watts* (Oak Harbor, WA: Logos Research Systems, Inc., 1998).

8. Charles H. Spurgeon, "Christ's Joy and Ours" (Sermon #2935).

9. A. W. Tozer, *Life in the Spirit* (Peabody, MA: Hendrickson, 2009), 153.

10. Greg Forster, *The Joy of Calvinism: Knowing God's Personal, Unconditional, Irresistible, Unbreakable Love* (Wheaton, IL: Crossway, 2012), 147–48.

11. Ricardo Sanchez, *It's Not Over* (Lake Mary, FL: Charisma House Book Group, 2012), 144.

12. Elizabeth George, *Walking with the Women of the Bible: A Devotional Journey through God's Word* (Eugene, OR: Harvest House, 1999), 28.

13. Spurgeon, quoted in Paul Lee Tan, *Encyclopedia of 7700 Illustrations* (Garland, TX: Bible Communications, 1996).

14. Jonathan Edwards, "The Church's Marriage to Her Sons, and to Her God," *The Works of Jonathan Edwards*, vol. 2.

15. Edwards, "Wherein the Zealous Promoters of This Work Have Been Injuriously Blamed," *The Works of Jonathan Edwards*, vol. 1.

16. Spurgeon, "A Happy Christian" (Sermon #736).

17. Spurgeon, "The Keynote of the Year" (Sermon #2121).

18. Spurgeon, "Two Immutable Things" (Sermon #2438).

19. Spurgeon, "Joy, A Duty" (Sermon #2405).

20. Mike Mason, *Champagne for the Soul: Celebrating God's Gift of Joy* (Vancouver, BC: Regent College, 2003), 31.
21. Joni Eareckson Tada, *Joni and Friends Daily Devotional*, November 28, 2013.

CHAPTER 6: DOES BLESSED MEAN HAPPY?

1. Randy Alcorn, *Happiness* (Carol Stream, IL: Tyndale House, 2015).
2. See *asher* in Francis Brown, ed., with S. R. Driver and Charles A. Briggs, *A Hebrew and English Lexicon of the Old Testament*, trans. Edward Robinson (Oxford: Clarendon, 1952); David J. A. Clines, ed., *Dictionary of Classical Hebrew*, vol. 1 (Sheffield, UK: Sheffield Phoenix Press, 1993); Ludwig Koehler, Walter Baumgartner, and Johan Jakob Stamm, *The Hebrew and Aramaic Lexicon of the Old Testament*, vol. 1 (Leiden, Netherlands: E. J. Brill, 1994).
3. *Merriam-Webster Unabridged Dictionary* (Britannica Digital Learning, 2014), s.v. "blessed," http://www.merriam-webster.com/thesaurus/blessed?show=0&t=1374098168.
4. Noah Webster, *An American Dictionary of the English Language*, vol. 1 (New York: S. Converse, 1828), 273.
5. Barclay M. Newman and Eugene A. Nida, *A Handbook on the Gospel of John*, UBS Handbook Series (New York: United Bible Societies, 1980), 437.

CHAPTER 7: WHERE DOES TRUE HAPPINESS BEGIN?

1. Richard L. Bushman, ed., *The Great Awakening: Documents on the Revival of Religion, 1740–1745* (Chapel Hill: University of North Carolina Press, 1989), 30.
2. Richard Sibbes, *The Complete Works of Richard Sibbes*, 4:136.
3. Thomas Traherne, "The First Century," *Centuries of Meditations*, no. 29.
4. Helen H. Lemmel, "Turn Your Eyes upon Jesus," 1922.
5. Jonathan Edwards, "His Early and Rapturous Sense of Divine Things."

6. George MacDonald, *An Expression of Character: The Letters of George MacDonald* (Grand Rapids, MI: Eerdmans, 1994), 18.

7. Quentin Fottrell, "This Is the Atheist Capital of America," *The Beer Barrel,* January 31, 2016, http://thebeerbarrel.net /threads/this-is-the-atheist-capital-of-america.34527/.

8. David Murray, "7 Kinds of Happiness," *HeadHeartHand* (blog), September 17, 2014, http://headhearthand.org/blog/2014/09 /17/7-types-of-happiness/.

9. Jennie says that as a little girl, she was very proud of her older brother, and she didn't even know he had competed in the Olympics until after his victory: Sheila Macgregor, "Olympic Games—Setting the Record Straight," *Blogging with Sheila* (blog), July 22, 2012, https://bloggingwithsheila.wordpress .com/2012/07/22/olympic-games-setting-the-record -straight/.

10. *Chariots of Fire*, directed by Hugh Hudson (Twentieth Century Fox, 1981).

11. Ibid.

CHAPTER 8: WHAT KILLS OUR HAPPINESS?

1. Timothy Keller, *Counterfeit Gods: The Empty Promises of Money, Sex, and Power, and the Only Hope That Matters* (New York: Dutton, 2009), xi–xii.

2. C. S. Lewis, *The Screwtape Letters* (New York: HarperCollins, 2001), 118.

3. John Piper, "We Want You to Be a Christian Hedonist!" *Desiring God*, August 31, 2006, http://www.desiringgod.org/Resource Library/Articles/ByDate/2006/1797_We_Want_You.

CHAPTER 9: IS IT OKAY TO FIND HAPPINESS IN GOD'S GIFTS?

1. John Calvin, *Institutes of the Christian Religion*, trans. Henry Beveridge, Book Second, chapter 2, "Man Now Deprived of Freedom of Will, and Miserably Enslaved."

2. A. W. Tozer, *The Attributes of God*, vol. 1 (Camp Hill, PA: WingSpread, 2007), 10, 12–13.

3. Randy Alcorn, *Heaven* (Carol Stream, IL: Tyndale House, 2004), 52.

4. *Babette's Feast*, directed by Gabriel Axel (Panorama Films, 1987).

5. William G. Morrice, *We Joy in God* (London: SPCK, 1977), 52.

6. Charles H. Spurgeon, "To Those Who Feel Unfit for Communion" (Sermon #2131).

CHAPTER 10: WHAT KEY UNLOCKS HAPPINESS?

1. D. Martyn Lloyd-Jones, *Studies in the Sermon on the Mount* (Grand Rapids, MI: Eerdmans, 1976), 102.

2. Stephen Charnock, "The Necessity of Regeneration," *The Complete Works of Stephen Charnock*, vol. 3.

3. Charles H. Spurgeon, "Sorrow and Sorrow" (Sermon #2691).

4. Spurgeon, "The Secret of Happiness" (Sermon #3227).

5. Martin Luther, "Sermon for the 19th Sunday after Trinity," *Sermons of Martin Luther*.

CHAPTER 11: IS HAPPINESS FOR NOW OR LATER . . . OR BOTH?

1. Calvin Miller, *The Taste of Joy: Recovering the Lost Glow of Discipleship* (Downers Grove, IL: InterVarsity Press, 1983), 18.

2. Charles H. Spurgeon, "Repentance after Conversion" (Sermon #2419).

CHAPTER 12: CAN WE BE HAPPY DESPITE SUFFERING?

1. Ann Voskamp, *One Thousand Gifts: A Dare to Live Fully Right Where You Are* (Grand Rapids, MI: Zondervan, 2010), 33.

2. Duncan Matheson, as quoted in C. R. Hurditch, ed., *Footsteps of Truth*, vol. 1 (London: J. F. Shaw, 1883), 393.

CHAPTER 13: WILL WE REALLY LIVE HAPPILY EVER AFTER?

1. Seneca, as quoted by David G. Myers, *Psychology*, 6th ed. (New York: Worth, 2001), 484.

2. A. W. Tozer and H. Verploegh, *The Quotable Tozer II: More Wise Words with a Prophetic Edge* (Camp Hill, PA: Christian Publications, 1997), 103.

3. Charles H. Spurgeon, "Christ's Joy and Ours" (Sermon #2935).

4. C. S. Lewis, *The Last Battle* (New York: HarperTrophy, 1994), 228.

5. Calvin Miller, *The Divine Symphony* (Minneapolis: Bethany House, 2000), 139.

6. Richard Baxter and William Orme, "The Divine Life: Walking with God," *The Practical Works of the Rev. Richard Baxter*, vol. 13.

7. Victor Hugo, "The Future Life," quoted in Dave Wilkinson, "And I Shall Dwell" (sermon, Moorpark Presbyterian Church, Moorpark, CA, February 18, 2001).

CHAPTER 14: HOW CAN HAPPINESS TRANSFORM US, OUR FAMILIES, AND THE CHURCH?

1. John Calvin, *Commentary on the Book of Psalms*, vol. 2, Psalm 37:27-29.

2. Thomas Aquinas, *Summa Theologica*, Prima Secundae Partis, question 5, article 4.

3. W. Gesenius and S. P. Tregelles, *Gesenius' Hebrew-Chaldee Lexicon to the Old Testament* (Bellingham, WA: Logos Research Systems, 2003).

4. James Swanson, *A Dictionary of Biblical Languages with Semantic Domains: Hebrew (Old Testament)* (Oak Harbor, WA: Logos Research Systems, 1997).

5. *The A. W. Tozer Bible (King James Version)* (Peabody, MA: Hendrickson, 2012), 1086.

6. Charles H. Spurgeon, "A Message to the Glad and the Sad" (Sermon #2546).

7. A. W. Tozer, *Who Put Jesus on the Cross?* (Camp Hill, PA: WingSpread, 2009), e-book.

8. Spurgeon, "Titles of Honor" (Sermon #3300).

About the Author

RANDY ALCORN is an author and the founder and director of Eternal Perspective Ministries (EPM), a nonprofit organization dedicated to teaching principles of God's Word and assisting the church in ministering to unreached, unfed, unborn, uneducated, unreconciled, and unsupported people around the world. His ministry focus is communicating the strategic importance of using our earthly time, money, possessions, and opportunities to invest in need-meeting ministries that count for eternity. He accomplishes this by analyzing, teaching, and applying biblical truth.

Before starting EPM in 1990, Randy served as a pastor for fourteen years. He has a bachelor of theology and a master of arts in biblical studies from Multnomah University and an honorary doctorate from Western Seminary in Portland, Oregon, and has taught on the adjunct faculties of both.

A *New York Times* bestselling author, Randy has

written more than fifty books, including *Heaven*, *The Treasure Principle*, and the award-winning novel *Safely Home*. Over ten million copies of his books have sold, and his titles have been translated into more than seventy languages. All royalties from his books are given to the works of Christian ministries, including world missions and organizations that care for the poor.

Randy has written for many magazines, including EPM's *Eternal Perspectives*. He is active on Facebook and Twitter and has been a guest on more than eight hundred radio, television, and online programs, including *Focus on the Family*, *FamilyLife Today*, and *Revive Our Hearts*.

Randy resides in Gresham, Oregon, with his wife, Nanci. They have two married daughters and are the proud grandparents of five grandsons. Randy enjoys time spent with his family, biking, underwater photography, research, and reading.

You may contact Eternal Perspective Ministries at www.epm.org or 39085 Pioneer Blvd., Suite 206, Sandy, OR 97055 or 503-668-5200. Follow Randy on Facebook and Twitter @randyalcorn and on his blog at www.epm.org/blog.

Scripture Sources
and Permissions

Think God doesn't want
you to be happy?

Think again.

Join noted theologian Randy Alcorn as he shows us
how we can experience all the happiness God has
to offer in *Happiness*, *God's Promise of Happiness*,
and *60 Days of Happiness*. These books will forever
change the way you think about happiness.

BOOKS BY RANDY ALCORN

FICTION

Deadline
Dominion
Deception
Edge of Eternity
Eternity
Lord Foulgrin's Letters
The Ishbane Conspiracy
Safely Home
Courageous
The Chasm

CHILDREN'S

Heaven for Kids
Wait Until Then
Tell Me About Heaven

STUDY GUIDES

The Grace and Truth Paradox Study Guide
The Treasure Principle Study Guide
The Treasure Principle Bible Study
The Purity Principle Study Guide
If God Is Good Study Guide
The Heaven Small Group Discussion Guide
The Heaven Workbook

NONFICTION

Happiness
God's Promise of Happiness
Does God Want Us to Be Happy?
Heaven
Touchpoints: Heaven
50 Days of Heaven
In Light of Eternity
Managing God's Money
Money, Possessions, and Eternity
The Law of Rewards
ProLife Answers to ProChoice Arguments
Sexual Temptation: Guardrails for the Road to Purity
The Goodness of God
The Grace and Truth Paradox
The Purity Principle
The Treasure Principle
Why ProLife?
If God Is Good . . .
The Promise of Heaven
We Shall See God
90 Days of God's Goodness
Life Promises for Eternity
Eternal Perspectives
Everything You Always Wanted to Know about Heaven
hand in Hand
Help for Women Under Stress
The Resolution for Men
Seeing the Unseen
Does the Birth Control Pill Cause Abortions?

CP0143